T0194002

< Another Perspective >

< Another Perspective >

Ellie Rose

< ANOTHER PERSPECTIVE >

iUniverse books may be ordered through booksellers or by contacting:

iUniverse
1663 Liberty Drive
Bloomington, IN 47403
www.iuniverse.com
1-800-Authors (1-800-288-4677)

Because of the dynamic nature of the Internet, any web addresses or links contained in this book may have changed since publication and may no longer be valid. The views expressed in this work are solely those of the author and do not necessarily reflect the views of the publisher, and the publisher hereby disclaims any responsibility for them.

Any people depicted in stock imagery provided by Getty Images are models, and such images are being used for illustrative purposes only. Certain stock imagery © Getty Images.

ISBN: 978-1-5320-9901-4 (sc)
ISBN: 978-1-5320-9902-1 (e)

Print information available on the last page.

iUniverse rev. date: 04/22/2020

Contents

CONTENTS

Dedicated to those who relate

< Prologue >

All I wanted was to be loved, but I got this instead.

Silas: "When will you ever learn! Always making the same mistakes. You dumb girl! This is your last warning you're so ungrateful. So selfish! Do you know how many people and children don't have a roof over their heads? Can't believe you're my child! Don't act like your mom! The Devil is always trying to steal my peace and ruin the holiday."

the door gets slammed shut

the words "Don't act like your mother" rang through my head

Ellie: *mumbles* .... "who said I was living comfortably in this house.... I- I'm selfish ... but, I never asked for any of it. I didn't ask for this house, this roof over my head, this pain..... and it's not like it was my wish to come into this shitty world. I know this pain and suffering will never go away so there's no point in wishing. I wish to leave this world by accident or purpose, but I can't even do that, because if I do it on purpose... "I'll go to hell."; and supposedly these people are Christians. 'The Devil is always trying to steal my peace...' You may not be Satan but you are a devil yourself and if anything; I'm already living hell."

~WHAT A PERFECT FAMILY.

< To be replaced >

It's Christmas. The one of many holidays I dislike most nowadays. Easter's alright, but why should I be celebrating someone's birthday that caused all this chaos leaving without guilt. Besides, I don't like it when my parents give me presents not because I don't like celebrating my birthday, Christmas, or because they love me, but because I know every time they give me a present they're indirectly saying to pay them back when I'm older. I'm sure of it. All those old scumbag's want is my money and for me to be a cardiologist or neurologist to make even more money for them. I hate celebrating in general. School break means I have to be with the Devil and his apprentice longer and the longer I stay with them the more problems we have as they judge my every move. That's really the only reason why I like school; Staying away from my parents and this "home sweet home" hell cage, and last, but not least I get to see my crush and my three friends; Ava, Lucinda, and Graye.

Aurora: "Wake up. It's Christmas." I thought it was Valentine's Day.

Ellie: *sarcastically* "Yeah, Merry Christmas!"

1

Aurora: "A day where we get to celebrate Jesus's Birthday is always a Blessed day. You are ready to go to school tomorrow."

Ellie: "Yeah."

Aurora: "Nothing much, We ran out of bread, quickly, get ready. I'll need your help getting groceries."

Ellie: "Hm, the one time I'm actually important."

She makes small chats along the way, and wishes she didn't. I prefer silence over her talking. Since every time she opens her mouth I'm worried my reply may provoke her.

Aurora: "You know, I was talking to a customer, she was going on and on about her son not caring for her. He may have a family but he can't just leave her like that. He just carried on, she must be so lonely in a senior home."

Ellie: "What was he posed to do."

Aurora: "Take care of her! That's his mom, he may have a family but she can stay with him meanwhile."

Ellie: "Considering he has a family, he can't take care of her."

Aurora: "He can have a nurse and in the meantime have her live in his household." *she clicks the signal*

Ellie: "They have many activities, she may have friends her age. You'll be going there soon enough."

Aurora: "No? I didn't raise someone for 18 years just to go to a senior home."

I sink in my seat

< Another Perspective >

Ellie: "Not like you did it well enough."

Aurora: "The audacity you have."

My teeth pulling at my lip I look at her for a silent moment and mumble Ellie: "The abhor you have."

opens door Ellie: "Hello dad."

Silas: "Hello Ellie, Merry Christmas."

Ellie: "Merry Christmas, to you too."

I grimace at how cringey my family is Silas: "Please pray for this blessing Ellie."

Ellie: "Okay, let's pray. Dear Lord Jesus, Thank you for this day. Even though I didn't wish to live. Thank you for all that you've done. Yeah all the misery you gave me. Thank you for always being with us and by our side. You were never on my side. That you give us this daily bread and deliver us from the evil one. Aren't you the evil one Amen."

Aurora: "Amen." Silas: "Amen."

Nothing spectacular here. Just a normal totally perfect christian family filled with hypocrites, but I can't complain.

I'm a hypocrite too.

< Safe Haven >

The only thing that might make me happy for a momentary time; well better than "home" at least; most kids would think I'm crazy, but something that makes me forget about what I'm going through would be heaven at the most and to me that's School. I just need to not get in trouble and maintain good grades so my parents won't have to go to school or have anything to do with it. I also get to see my crush and most of all, my friend's.

pictures flash

Even though I know they'll leave me one day just like everyone else.

Aurora: "Ellie, Wake Up! You're late for school. I told you to set your alarm for 6:00 a.m."

Ellie: "Sorry, I guess I slept through the alarm."

Aurora: "Don't lie to me. You're not much of a heavy sleeper. Are you dead or what?!" I Wish.

Aurora: "Hurry up! You have five minutes!" Ellie: "Okay, okay I get it."

get ready

goes to car

wait's for mom

sighs

Ellie: "Hah." *mumbles* "It's funny how she always yells at me to hurry up and when i'm ready i'd have to wait for her."

Whatever, I'm going to school. I don't want to start the day bad. I should at least be happy once in a few times to the point of life.

mom walks into garage

opens door to car

starts engine

Aurora: "Did you do all your homework?"

Ellie: "Yes, I have."

Aurora: *looks at me through the rear-view mirror* "As expected you need outstanding grades to get a well paid career like a cardiologist or neurologist. It's what's best for you."

I look down with a distraught face

Ellie: "Why can't I ever choose the way my life goes or in this case my career?"

Aurora: "What are you trying to say?" *mom looks at me through the corner of her eye*

< Another Perspective >

She never looks at me directly neither does my dad, but I'm actually quite glad, because when they ever do it's when they're mad and it's like I can see the fire flaking in their eyes wishing the worst upon me.

Ellie: "I mean... you know, decide my own future."

I've never spoken my mind, always scared they wouldn't even bear to listen and if they did so they would quickly reject my own ideology as this being my first I was appalled.

mom looks at me with a straight disappointed face
Aurora: "No!"

mom alters into a triggered emotion

frightened by her sudden change of emotion I start to quiver

mom seems to snap out of her sudden expression into a calm happy face

Aurora: "...I don't think that's meant to be, sweetie. A mother knows what's best for their child."

scared to speak a word I just nod in disbelief of what just went on

drives to school

drifts to school entrance

Aurora: "I believe this is where you get off at." *she smiles*

Ellie: "yeah, thanks for driving me; see ya'"

Aurora: "Okay. Bye, I Love you"

7

Ellie: "Bye"

Aurora: "I Love You"

You lie a lot. You know that. Ellie: *opens door*

But I shouldn't provoke her for that.

Ellie: "Yeah..I like you too, bye"

Because I lie too. Aurora: "Bye"

closes door

I don't understand why she's faking it and it's totally obvious to me...... Who cares for now. At Least I got eleven hours away from the devil and his apprentice. Besides you have Ava, Lucinda, Graye to support you, but you can't rely on them all the time. Now that I think about it; that's kinda sad, trapped; counting the dates until you're free. Whenever that is.

smile

Ellie: "It's alright girl, you got this just get through with it for five more years it might go by quicker than you think just have hope. Just five more years of pain and suffering. Then it will all be over." *I say to myself trying to boost my ego*

Just five more years.

I walk toward the cafeteria as someone yells across the hall
Ava: "Ellie!! Over here!" *waves hand*

Lucinda and Ava wait for me near the bleachers

Ellie: *walks towards Ava and Lucinda* "Hey...where's Graye?"

8

< Another Perspective >

Ava: "He texted me that he'll be absent today."

Ellie: "Damn. Sucks to hear, it's boring without him..."

Lucinda: "aww...you like him."

Ellie: "... you know I like Skylar." Ava: "Yeah, Skylar's hella cute!"

Lucinda: ",but you know it seems like he likes you by the way he looks at you."

Ellie: "He looks at me the same way he looks at everyone else; with his nonchalant face and brooding eyes."

Lucinda: "I know, I know I'm only teasing."

It's wild to me how Graye would hang with us.

I look down

Ava: "You're late." *smiles* "I've been starting to miss your face."

Ellie: "Well you can have it. I'd probably be prettier as a Slender man's wife."

we laugh

Ava: "Soooo~ how was Winter break." Ellie: "Pretty decent as always"

Ellie: *slight smile* "How was your's." Ava: "'Got to go to Seattle for a week."

Lucinda: "I went to a family reunion and got fatter." Ellie: "wow, both sounds interesting."

Ava: *smirks* "Oh, did you eat breakfast yet?"

Ellie: "No, it's alright. I wasn't feeling hungry anyways, I'm never hungry for school food."

bell ring's

DINNN~ DINN~

DINNN~

Ava: *sighs* "I didn't even get to talk with you and the first period is about to begin. Don't masterbate in Mrs.Oaks class over Skylar." *grins*

Ellie: "Be quiet" *giggles* "Besides Cheer up! I'll be able to see you in the 3rd period not long from now."

Ava: "Lucinda's lucky she has all periods with you."

Ellie: "Yeah I know, I always leave school with a headache." *jocking I grin*

Lucinda: "True, I love bothering Ellie."

I bet everyone does.

Ava: "At second thought, You're right. I'll see you soon don't want to be late to class." *walks to class as she looks behind waving at me*

Ellie: "You might want to look forward, you're close to hitting a pole."

< Another Perspective >

Lucinda: I actually wish you didn't tell her so she could hit the pole"

Ava: *looks straight away an inch from the pole* "Oh shit, close call, good thing if I did get hit you guys would be there for me to comfort and cuddle with."

Lucinda: *acts sarcastic* "No...not really...I wouldn't be there" *giggles*

Ellie: "Heh. Yeah, we'd be there for you. Byeeee~"

Lucinda: "PEACE~" *she says as she throws the peace sign*

Ava: "Bye"

To Be honest there are some reasons to live in this world, but the majority of reason's are bad. It's starting to change in my view or more like it was always like that i'm just starting to see it clearly now. Though good reasons to actually consider living for are vanishing before me and soon will I. I kind of get it though, it's like a stranded light around a flock of darkness; it's too weak and will give up or join the darkness. So world; when you find me dead you better be happy, saying im "selfish" or would you rather have me shoot and kill a percentage of humanity i'll gladly do that you're lucky i'm being considerable leaving you at rest, because you're indirectly killing me right now for more than ten years and i'm sick and tired of it! I lost myself, but didn't even know who I was to begin with one voice saying I'm normal and so is the situation I'm in. It will just go away like every other thing that passes by while the other is screaming in agony as I try to ignore it. I feel like I'm having a nightmare disorder, but in real life it's reality. Actually I think it would rather be better to have nightmares at least it will only hurt me mentally rather than mentally and physically.

< Test Me >

Ellie: "Hey, You up?"

Graye: "No not really."

Ellie: "You said you're here for me so I wanted to, I don't know get some frozen yogurt and chill?"

Graye: "I don't remember saying that, If so I take it back. I'm messing, but why frozen yogurt and at 10?"

Ellie: "It's great and why not."

Graye: "Sure thing. I'll pick you up."

Ellie: "No, we can walk. I wanna just wander around. I have time to spare."

Graye: "Well I don't. Let's remember we have school tomorrow. I'm joking again."

I make a small fake laugh

Graye: "Don't pity laugh at me. Haha, It'll be cooled anyways so we can waste time in my car."

Ellie: "Ok thanks."

I change my clothes to a warm outfit with no obsessive thoughts in my mind

I hear him pull to the curb and I hope my fence met with the passenger door open and music spewing out

Graye: "How was your few moments of sleep."

Ellie: "I didn't go to sleep."

Graye: "What were you up to?"

Ellie: "Contemplating and thinking if I should call you or not, I was also imagining how great frozen yogurt would be."

Graye: "What's wrong?"

I look at him as he focus on the road

Ellie: "What's never wrong in my life."

Graye: "Waking up a friend to get frozen yogurt doesn't sound so wrong to me."

Ellie: "My parents got into an argument about something I don't even know. The usual."

Graye: "Sorry to hear, frozen yogurts the way to go."

we get out of the car puting diabetes ontu our cup topped with fruit

We head back to the car he turns on the heater

< Another Perspective >

Graye: "Do they argue a lot?"

Ellie: "Ever so often, when they do though, It lasts awhile. I don't know what made them think it was a good decision to get married."

Graye: "They must've not thought it out, Just like how they argue for little things as you said."

Ellie: "Yeah, I feel pressured by them to have great grades and go to a great school for the best future. They mask themselves to be so wise and they both made the decision to get married and ruin each other's lives."

Graye: "That's on them, don't think about it so much,"

Ellie: "I get dragged anyways, they're so petty. My dad loves the idea of being right no matter what so as soon as there's a problem it seems like he tells me his side of the story to seem like he's done nothing wrong. I don't know who to blame though."

Graye: "Why not put it on both of them."

Ellie: "I think my mom feels like without us there's nothing else. Like she'd feel as if she wasted her adult years just to leave after realizing so lately. She probably just wanted to be loved and doesn't have the courage to do so. My father has his own problems as a kid that brought him to life style. She doesn't stick up for me though. She knows he has problems, but she sticks to his side even then."

Graye: "They should pray it out."

Ellie: "Their christians but they don't agree much and everythings toxic. They both say the other one isn't a true christian. My dad has anger issues, my moms bipolar and there's me depressed with a side of anxiety."

Graye: "Maybe things will be over when they hear it from you."

Ellie: "I highly doubt it. I'm sure my mom may be shocked and happy since she couldn't do it even at her age, but he has this inferiority complex and like I said. He likes to be right. He'd probably kick me out of the house, I wouldn't graduate in this area or see you. If he doesn't he'll blow up in my face about how great of a Father he is until he finally calms down and ignores me with this whole attitude and it would be awkward until I leave his house at my own will."

Graye: "So what's your plan?"

Ellie: "To wait things out until I'm legally capable of being on my own. Then I can tell him off and never see them again. They just push me off too often. I feel so tested that I'm walking on eggshells in my own house, but Maybe they were meant to be."

Graye: "I guess it's best to wait if you're capable of enduring for so long."

Ellie: "I hope so. I hope your lifes going great?"

Graye: "Um yeah, a bit. My dads getting himself together I'd like to say, Maybe I should get him some Frozen yogurt to celebrate."

we guffaw

Graye: "I'm sure he'd prefer alcohol though. Well see how long things last."

< Another Perspective >

Ellie: "Hopefully a while so we can do stuff like this more often."

Graye: "Yeah. Long enough for Ava, Lucinda, You, and I to go to the same highschool and graduate together."

Ellie: "Sounds amazing."

< Alright then >

A day where I don't have to worry about a single thing, getting stressed out. I don't need a vacation or a "Best day of my life" statement. I just want to relax and have a calm mind. There's no true point for me to live anymore out of seven days in the week only a few are happy, but those days are still contaminated with sadness. At this point I'm in Idleness just wanting time to pass without me doing much of anything, because any move I make can bring me even more misery than I already have. I can't be happy without keeping my guard up at all times, because it's come to the point that I'm afraid of being happy, because as soon as I am something horribly bad happens. Seems like everyone says "people out in the world are having it worse" so what can I do but smile when my problems are just the tip of an Iceberg.

Quite Ironic that I don't take my own advice which I give to others. How funny ellie how you yourself doesn't take her own advice you're always trying to help and out of all of this you don't even take that advice in. Just last for five more years and you'll be eighteen and most of the burden on your shoulders will be lifted. You're fine. It's okay."-

Aurora: "Hey" *waves* "I'm over here"

walks into car

Silas: "How was school, did you learn anything new?"

Ellie: "Umm... yeah I did..."

Aurora: "How are your grades?"

Ellie: *lies* "All A's."

Aurora: "...It's Decent"

Fuck, I should have said all A+ instead she would believe that.

Aurora: "Did you do your homework?"

Ellie: "Yes...as always."

awkward silence

reaches home

Ellie: "Thanks, for the ride."

opens door to house

This is my normal routine parent's curious about my grade's daily not because they love me, but since they are greedy they like making sure that I'm not too much of a failure wasting all their time. Dad yells at me and argues with mom as soon as he comes from work. The act's like our family is the best and is nice to me even though there may be an excuse for the stupidest reasons and mom takes dad's side whenever she can, because you know she's scared too. One of my motives is to be quick and stay out of dads way, but make sure to not make a mistake, especially while trying to be quick.

< Another Perspective >

dad opens door

Silas: "Hello."

Ellie: "Hello."

Silas: "How was school today?"

Being around dad you have to say what he wants to hear. If it's not even near the perspective he wants well you won't be pleased with the results.

Ellie: "School was good today."

Silas: "Say it was blessed today, not good everyday is a blessing." If this man doesn't shut the fuck up-

Ellie: "School was blessed today."

Silas: "Good to hear."

Well obviously. It's what you want to hear. Silas: "How are your grades?"

Ellie: "All A's" *lies again*

Silas: "All A's?! Is there no such thing as A+" *sarcastic smile* "Don't you know that I work twenty four seven for you and all the money goes to Vacation! Don't make me upset! You must be good at something else since you're not great in school. All you have to do is get all A+ in your classes is that so hard!" *puts hand on forehead* "Please just go prepare dinner, Let me take a shower."

I don't know how many times I'll mention this but just again both my parents are like this but it's not because they care

for me or my future just so they can take my money and use my successes as a luxury. My mom just follows him like a lost puppy that can't see the light and he just uses her because he loves the thought of everyone looking down before him. He's in denial because he was not the ideal family he wants, but he makes sure we plaster a smile on the outside. The devil and his apprentice.

Ellie: "Okay"

clenches fist

the nails digging into my palm

Great job you only had to eat dinner and be with him for an hour and ruined that. You fuckin' asshole! You should have said you have all A+ 's, but it's easier said than done he's complaining about me having just all A's if he realizes you're real grade even though it's good he won't be pleased. Just go prepare dinner. Only one hour until you go to sleep. Only five years 'till you turn eighteen and get the hell out of this place. You can do fine, suffer all this shit and be free at 18. You've already been through thirteen years of it. What can five more years do?

eats dinner surrounded by awkward silence

finishes dinner first

starts washing dishes

Silas: "Thank you, for washing the dishes if you continue doing chores and practicing like this you'll be prepared for future terms."

Ellie: "Your welcome."

< Another Perspective >

You mean if I continue being a slave you've worked me so hard I don't even look forward to the future anymore and what do you mean by future i'll i'm doing is living your life I'm a pawn in this world a game of chess I would say. That's how it usually goes. He yells at me and acts like everything's fine while I'm scared screaming at the top of my lungs inside my head in agony; he probably thinks it's the right way of teaching a child, always bragging that he has the best daughter on the phone to other parents. He brags for his ego not because he's truly happy with me, I'm his prize that's mistreated.

progenitors on-going conversation

Silas: "Hey Aurora, did you know that Talon's brother, Isaac died."

Aurora: "Really?! I had no idea; he was so young. How did he die?"

Silas: "From what I heard he commited suicide"

mom gasps

Aurora: "Oh my, Why?! That's so unexpected of him. Yet only 26. Does he know that you'll go to hell if you commit suicide?"

Silas: "I don't even know if he knew Jesus. I wasn't really friends with him, but his brother Talon. That's so unfair it's going to be christmas in four days and he died before the holiday. He ruined it for everyone now his family will mourn every christmas at his death. How rude to die near Christmas and ruin everyone's happiness."

Aurora: "How sad he thought that he would find peace dieing, but committing suicide will only take you to hell." *shakes her head in disappointment* "Will there be a funeral?"

Silas: "Yes, They have invited us to the event. It will be held Sunday April 22, 2018 at 8:30."

Aurora: "Why so early?!"

You shouldn't be complaining besides you're not the one who lost someone not like you'd care anyways and bitch I wake up every day at six for school or six thirty if I'm late. You can handle this.

Silas: "Since we both don't go to work and have no plans on that day, we all can attend the funeral, as a family."

continues to wash the dishes

Disgusting. Is that all you can say and think about? He must have been suffering to make that decision and come to the conclusion to take his own life. I understand his family may be busy and such, but if you really cared for him you would notice the slightest mix in his mood he had so i'm actually not sorry to the family for their loss they should have paid more attention he was still under them since he was seventeen. They shouldn't have given birth if they can't even pay attention to a child and my parents over here are only caring about my future and the money and success you'll get. What about the present, because without that, there will be no future. Now I know that if-...when I die from suicide that's what you'll think. That's fine with me. I'm Just a nonentity. That most will forget.

finishes washing dishes

Ellie: "Goodnight mom, goodnight dad."

Silas: "Goodnight."

Aurora: "Goodnight, have a nice dream."

24

< Another Perspective >

Ellie: "'night."

As I rethink everything that's been around lately I've come to realize that I don't care if I go to hell from dying. At some point I guess I would rather kill myself and get punished by the devil rather than emotionally breaking down everyday getting punished for something that i've never done or for a worthless reason. I bet God is laughing at me suffering thinking I'm stuck in his little game having to suffer. He knew that we would think of killing ourselves so he made it a foul in the game and would punish us if we killed ourselves. Well guess what, go ahead and punish me. I don't care. I haven't cared about anything in a long time. So punish me; isn't that what you've been doing all this time? In fact, maybe when i'm in hell i'll get to ask the devil why everyone hates me, maybe then I will get the true answer. I always look forward to night time. Most are calm. I don't talk to my parents. No screaming or problems and even though I don't get to see my friends or crush. I get to live a fantasy even though it won't save me for a long time. Well besides Splendering. That place has one of the best foods.

Ellie: "ugh. It's already six o'clock" *feels forehead* "It was just a dream- no that was a nightmare."

changes uniform

Ellie: "Damn, It's bad enough reality is a living hell, but now I'm haunted in my sleep too. Just great."

Aurora: *startled* "Oh, you finally woke up on time." *she says sarcastically*

Ellie: "well, yeah...it was only a one time thing, I guess.."

Aurora: "Good, I have to go early to work today. The schedules changed, so you're going to have to walk to the bus."

You don't have to lie. I know you're going to go smoke like you always do.

Ellie: "Okay, that's fine."

Aurora: "I'll see you later tonight."

Ellie: "Okay, bye."

Aurora: "Bye"

She didn't say "I love you" this time. Good, it was awkward the last time she said that bullshit. I hate the bus. There is hardly any room so I have to sit with three people in a seat as my ass is falling off the edge of the seat. Damn it. Well I guess it's better than having awkward moments in the car with my mom.

steps outside of house

Ellie: "Shit, I forgot my phone and keys."

runs upstairs

grabs phone and keys

Ellie: "I still have some time left before the bus comes, but I should get there before they leave too early."

door shuts

runs to the bus stop

bus leaves

Ellie: *mumbles in frustration* "Oh my God, did they really fucken' leave; that bitchy ass driver. She didn't care for the

< Another Perspective >

slightest reason, damn it. Those kids would have told the bus driver to wait."

"Oh are you here for the bus of Summit Institute Middle School. You just missed it, they came early today."

Ellie: "Yeah, I Know. It's alright." No, It's not alright.

"Alright." *whispers* "poor girl." *slowly walks away*

I kind of wished that lady would've given me a ride, but if my mom found out I would be in more trouble than her just finding out I missed the bus I'd be dead now that I'm not already, because I am dying inside. She wouldn't care, because it's a stranger or anything, but I guess she gets embarrassed making it seem like our family is homeless for some reason. She's ashamed of this family that's for sure. Besides getting rid of this pain by dying, if everyone found out how I died they would be disgusted and my parents would be more than embarrassed. I wish I could see that day but to make it happen in the first place I must die. There's nothing to lose really I'm just having a slight hope in humanity really.

Ellie: *mumbles* "This will be easy. All I have to do is walk to school. It's like 15 minutes away,......but that's by car."

Ellie: "Shit, out of all days. I should have run quicker...whatever it's fine as long as my mom doesn't find out then she'll be pissed that I missed the first period of school. It's not like I could stay home for the day just because I missed the bus."

Ellie: "...and dad he'll yell at me some more, it's better if they don't find out."

I walk hastily

Ellie: "Shit this is the worst time to rain i'll smell like a wet dog. I'm already a twig. Why do I have to sweat and suffer? I can't get any skinnier. I'm going to look like a drug addict bum by the time I reach school unless I don't reach school and some wild animal jumps out of a bush and eats me alive."

43 minutes later

Ellie: "Just great the day didn't even start and I smell like shit." *lowers voice* "I'm not really in a state of complaining. I guess it could have been worse. Music would take my mind off of this."

attempts powers on phone

Ellie: "Bro"

tries to power on phone again

Ellie: "Don't tell me..."

powers on phone again, again

Ellie: "This shitty ass flip phone is dead! Bruh I've been charging it all night." *I pull my hair back and sigh* "Forget it, stay calm Ellie, stay calm you don't want to die from stress.... Wait actually you want to because then "you're not selfish" and have a "good reason" for dying. It's fine you can go on for a few more minutes."

47 minutes later

reaches school

Ellie: *mumbles* "By a "few minutes" I didn't know it would take this long."

28

< Another Perspective >

opens door to office

Ellie: *mumbles under breath* "You must be a real bitch to not get well paid bus drivers; making me late to school."

Office Worker: "Good Morning"

Ha, I wonder how she'd feel If i said "you're supposed to say Blessed Morning everyday is blessed.

I mock my dads words in my head

Ellie: "Hey um..I believe I have to sign a paper saying I was tardy today."

Office Worker: "Okay, Just sign right here please." *looks at parking lot through window*

Ellie: *signs paper* "Okay, I've signed it."

Office Worker: "Now right below your signature why you're tardy." *points at bottom of slip*

Ellie: "The bus left me, literally."

Office Worker: *she reads my response* "You mean, you were late for the bus?"

Ellie: "No."

Office Worker: *looks confused*

Ellie: "What is written is exactly what happened. The bus left me" *talks under breath* "just how people have left and will leave me."

Office Worker: "Well, where are your parents?" Parents. Ha, yeah right they sure don't act like parents.

Ellie: "At work...you won't call them will you?"

Office Worker: "You walked here? This school is quite far from even the nearest resident area's."

You think. I try my best not to complain much so I keep it to myself all in my head, but can you at least tell the bus drivers to come on time and leave on time not early not late- no, no you can't say that to her then you'll be acting like you're dad that's the last thing you want. It's bad enough you have their blood. I just want to stab myself a billion times every time I think about it. It's disgusting. I'm disgusting.

Ellie: "Yeah, I walked here."

Office Worker: "Wow. Must have been quite far." "Quiet far" yeah damn right it was far.

Ellie: "Oh it wasn't that far by running at a pace it's only about one hour and twenty minutes."

I say sarcastically trying not to think about it holding my tears from crying in front of her I change the subject

Ellie: "What period are we in now?"

Office Worker: "Second"

Ellie: "I'll be on my way then."

opens door

I'm not saying I deserve a mansion, money, cars or anything

< Another Perspective >

like that, but I sure don't deserve this. This is the second time today people said "poor girl" to me. Do people really pity me that much? If she really thinks I'm suffering, what will she do? Kinda sad how lot's pity I have except the people that are supposed to. I wonder if they ever pitied me- ah who am I kidding they don't even care about me and if they even think about me then it must be a negative thought. Like them waiting for me to do something wrong so they could quickly correct me the second I step out of line. I can't forget to not make mistakes and be perfect. I can't afford it either.

a tear streams down I'm just so frustrated.

< Dim Light >

Ellie: *smiles* "Hey Graye."

Graye: "Hey Ellie."

walks to me waving his hand

Graye: "It's been a while."

Ellie: "Yeah, why were you absent yesterday?"

Graye: "Didn't feel like showin' up."

Lucky. My parents would never let me stay home even if I was sick. It's not like I even wanna' stay home. They would just make shit quality reasons to yell at me. A melancholy feeling suddenly sank inside of me as the thought of everyone enjoying life as time passes by, but I get to be stuck in time suffering in pain by faults I have never done and all I can do is look around at happy people swarmed inside my head.

Graye: "....What's wrong?"

Graye stops me with my thoughts

Ellie: "Huh, oh nothing, -Ava and Lucinda are here." *I smile as I start to walk toward Ava and Lucinda:*

Graye quickly, but gently grabs my right wrist

Graye: "I'm not trying to be nosy or anything, but....are you sure?"

Ellie: "Yeah, I'm fine."

Graye: "Just tell me...I'm here for you. I swear."

To think someone would even care the slightest about me.

Ellie: "I'm seriously fine, don't worry about me."

Graye: "Promise me you'll tell me anything. Even if it's about a girl drama I won't mind okay?"

Ellie: "Okay." *chuckle* "Haha, I promise."

Ava and Lucinda come half into the conversation

Ava: "Yay! The group is back." *Ava yells*

Graye: "Jeez, tone it down a notch you'll blow my eardrums real quick at this rate."

Lucinda: "You're Lucky you only have us in one period."

We all have some periods with each other, but there's one period where all of us are together. In Mrs.Provence's class with Skylar.

Ava: "Did you guys eat Breakfast already?"

< Another Perspective >

Graye: "Yeah."

Lucinda: "Yup."

Ellie: "No."

Ava: "Gosh Ellie you never eat. Thinkin' 'bout starving to death."

She's right, I'll be looking anorexic if this keeps up. Skylar I'd have a lower possibility with Skylar if that happens.

Ellie: "No.....but know that you've mentioned..."

Graye suddenly looks flabbergasted

Ava: "...I was joking, Ellie. I didn't really mean it."

Ellie: "I'm playing around too."

Ava: "Heh, we say the weirdest shit."

Lucinda: "So...um."

we all crackle an awkward laugh

Ava: "...Okay, now it's awkward, let's go eat."

walks to cafeteria

Ava and Lucinda lead the way leaving Graye and me a few steps behind

Graye: *In a low voice* "Hey Ellie, were you really joking about starving to death."

Ellie: "Yeah I was." *I say solemnly*

35

Graye: "You scare me quite a lot when you say things like that."

Ellie: *looking aghast* "I do?!"

Graye: "Heck yeah you do. You always give me heart attacks and ava with her loud voice blowing my eardrums as Lucinda's always hyper. I'll be old soon enough." *soft smile* "It might sound weird, but I actually like Ava's obnoxious personality, Lucinda's enthusiasm and you're dirty jokes. Even Lucinda when she acts sassy. I would be bored without it."

I reply back with a smile softy

he sighs to a sad calm face Ellie: "Something up?" *I ask*

Graye: *he closes his eyes nodding his head vertically* "Ugh, no. I was just thinking about something."

Ellie: "Something?" *I became curious to know*

Graye: "I was just wondering... would you care if I left?"

Ellie: "Left? What do you mean by that?"

Graye: "I mean if I moved."

Ellie: "I would celebrate with Ava and Lucinda."

Graye makes a frown face

Ellie: "Haha, I'm just kidding!"

Graye: "I know, you have a sense of humour only Ava, Lucinda, and I understand." *he smiles brightly with the warm sun gleaming his face* ",but I think I've hung around you for a

< Another Perspective >

while that I'm starting to understand too. How scary. *he gives a slight laugh*

my whole face turns bright red

Ellie: "U-um...I would probably feel sad. Why?"

Graye: "Just wondering., but if you need me or something just tell me, okay?."

I smile back

Ellie: "Okay."

eats breakfast

Knowing Graye he's never really smiled seeing his first made me honored especially since he's said he cared about me. I love Graye, Ava, and Lucinda all equally or at least I try too. I don't want to replace one with the other or make someone feel unwanted trust me feeling unwanted is never a good thing, but they both have the specialties Ava always makes me laugh and she's the "happy go lucky" type, Lucinda loves to laugh, but can be serious at some moments acting tough and sassy as Graye said. Graye on the other hand is usually never happy or mad. He's always calm and he never gets in trouble and is the popular dude that hangs out with "weird people" and he's actually quite shy in a way that makes him the mysterious type. He's the first and probably the last person to see right through me. He reads my dismal mind and knows my mood most of the time, but I have a limit to everything as he always asks "are you okay?" as I reply "I'm fine."

pant *huff*

Ellie: "why do we have to run again?" *breathes heavily*

37

Lucinda: "'Cuz our P.E teachers are some little bitches." *groans*

Ellie: "This is so unfair. I just ran like an hour to school as if there was a marathon."

Lucinda: "Life's unfair."

Ellie: "Well it should be, because one day if I tell my mom "Life's unfair" and shoot her, it's not like people will understand and let it pass by."

Lucinda: "Damn that was deep you say the weirdest things you know. Wait, you ran to school, you attempting to run away from home like you always planned?"

Ellie: "No I missed the bus, more like it left without me."

Lucinda: "Ha, that's sad no wonder you look shittier than you normally do."

Ellie: "Be quiet; besides I would never have the courage to run away what would become my life after that I'll die that way anyways.....unless you let me stay at your house."

Lucinda: "Hell no, my mom would never let that happen." Ellie: "..She doesn't have to know."

Lucinda: "Oh yeah that sounds like a good idea until she cleans my bedroom and finds someone sleeping in the closet."

Ellie: "Okay, Okay I get it."

Lucinda: "Is your mom really that mean?"

Ellie: "She's more than mean, it's not just her, but my dad too."

< Another Perspective >

I hate talking about my problems and stress. It makes me sound weak. Everyone has problems in their life; I shouldn't complain, So I pretend my family has arguments and normal problems like all the other families. Deep down I know it's not just a regular family problem. Though my family doesn't act like a "family".

Ellie: "It's not that bad, just regular problems we get over as a family." Lies after Lies piling up.

Lucinda: "I get it, my parents are annoying too. Always telling me to do shit."

Ellie: "Yeah, sort of like that.

I soon realized the slow pace we were taking making us the last ones left on the track field

Ellie: "Shit, we're the last ones to hurry up slowpoke."

I sprint looking back at her with a huge grin

Lucinda: "Wait! You know i'm obese, slow down!"

Ellie: ",and you know I'm a twig the wind will blow me any second. see ya' there."

Lucinda gives off a soft smile and races up to by my side

Lucinda: "Damn, Why is P.E so far from everything else we literally have no time to change and go to Mrs.Provence's class which is across the fucking campus."

Ellie: "Oh well, Life's unfair."

Lucinda: "Girl, shut up."

Ellie: "What did I do?!"

laugh

Ellie: "No, but seriously you're right. Everyday it's a hassle to get here on time in less than four minutes."

Lucinda: "Tell me about it, Literally."

Lucinda and I wave at Ava and Graye Mrs.Provence: "Settle down Scholars."

passes the students a sheet of paper

Mrs.Provence: "So today we'll be learning more about mental health and behaviours.." Ironic, This is one of the reasons why I like Mrs.Provence. I Learn with Interest. Mrs.Provence: "People don't really like talking or discussing this topic whether they have it or not or whether they like talking about it or not. It exists and you can't Ignore it. With the paper I have passed out to everyone I would like you to write what can make you have depression, why people don't talk about it from both perspectives, who you would go to if you were or are depressed and If you have depression or not. Don't be afraid no one will read, but me and I are very open minded. Now If you may, please start."

reads paper in my head

I see with the corner of my eye someone staring at me

I slightly turn my head to the left to see who it is Why's he staring at me?

Skylar notices that I notice him staring

< Another Perspective >

At that moment we both were directly staring at each other as if we were in a trans and we couldn't break out of it.

Skylar breaks the silence Skylar: "Hey, I'm Skylar."

I know.

Ellie: "Hey, I'm Ellie."

he reaches out his hand to me as a friendly gesture

I grab it to shake it shockingly at what's happening

I hear my friends quietly screaming in the background

If she doesn't shut the fuck up. Oh my gosh *I hold my laughter*

Mrs.Provence: "Okay you have one minute until the bell rings. Please turn in the paper as I will see you tomorrow."

Ava: "What the Fuck just happened, i'm happy for you.... You could have done more though, shit that was the best opportunity you could have asked if he was single!"

Lucinda: "You know Ellie, she likes taking things like this slowly."

both of them were super excited i'd say more excited than I was

Ava: "Give him a hug next time."

Ellie: "You know I'll never be able to do that."

Maybe there is Hope. Maybe there's a chance between Me and Skylar.

I see a flash of the student president with a frantic face as she stomps out of the class Does she always have to be so paranoid?

Ava: "Then you can kiss him goodbye, wait never mind forget kissing when you can't even hug, but seriously there's nothing to be afraid of I'll hook you up with him."

I'll never have confidence to do that. I lost something like that a long time ago, remember?

Ava quickly rushes to Skylar without my answer and before I had the chance to stop her she was already there making a fool of herself saying cheesy puns to Skylar making him laugh as Lucinda was laughing at how retarded Ava looked

Why do I get the feeling this has already happened Deja vu or what?

I automatically remember the nightmare I had last night Oh yeah, that's what this reminds me of.

,but being honest I didn't care anymore about the dream I had last night; It was just a dream and I was assured it would stay a dream; we turned in our paper, packed our stuff and headed out the door; people walking past looked at me awkwardly, but I get that, because from then on I was smiling from ear to ear; and I couldn't stop

< Just say it >

Graye: "You sure look happy."

I break out of my daydreams

Ellie: "Huh?! Oh yeah, I guess I am happy."

I look down and lightly blush

Graye: "Well, stop. It's creepy when you see a girl walking and just randomly smiles at the ground." *he smiles*

Damn he looks even better when he smiles. What the hell am I thinking I like Skylar?

Graye: "...What made you happy."

I froze there; muted like my vocals were just snatched

I never really told Graye how I felt about Skylar even though I told Ava and Clemin. I guess I just feel that he wouldn't understand, maybe I feel that way since he's a boy. No. I would be lying if that was the only reason. Me not telling him who I like is not the only reason to him being a boy.

43

I just can't figure out the real reason for myself.

Graye: ",but it's nice to see you happy and truly smile. That's a once in a lifetime sight to see. You should smile more, I like seeing you happy."

Ellie: "I'd say the same to you."

we both give of a warm smile as the sun is at dusk

Graye: "Um.. since we haven't been spending much time together mainly 'cuz I'm busy packing. I ugh... I mean since I haven't been to school lately."

his left hand grabs his right elbow as he stares at his shoes

Graye: "I don't know, I just thought maybe we could...go to the park?... I mean it's been awhile we spend alone time just the two of us... which was in what...6th grade when we had that science project You don't have to-"

Ellie: "Yeah, sounds good." *I smile*

Graye quickly looks up at me surprised

Graye: "Really?! I mean, yeah great."

Graye runs past the gate barely exiting the school

Ellie: "Where are you going?"

he turns half way around

Graye: "Race ya'"

Ellie: "Wait Are you serious? You got a head start!"

< Another Perspective >

I madly dash after him

Graye: "Damn, you're fast you had nothing to complain about me getting a head start."

I used to sneak out of the house when I was a kid to run at night yelling to let my anger out.

I soon surpass him; stopping at the nearest tree in the park

he sit laying his back to thegroung the breeze messes with his hair

Graye: "Ha, good race." *he says out of breath*

Ellie: "You're not so bad yourself."

I lay on the grass beside him

we both turn to each other just a few inches apart

our faces turn bright red as I quickly turn away

Ellie: "Sorry"

I usually never mean it when I say sorry, but I did.

Graye: "What for?"

Ellie: "I must make you worry a lot."

Graye: "Should I though."

I turn to look at him

Ellie: "No."

Graye: "Not like it's your fault. I just care for you. Like I do to all my friends."

Ellie: *I lightly smile* "Thanks."

I nudge him a little with my shoulder

Ellie: "If you need me...I'll be there for you too."

Graye turns bright red

Graye: "Ellie I-"

What were you about to say

Ellie: "You what?" *I tilt my head slightly* "What were you going to say?"

Graye: "Ugh nevermind" *he shakes his head* "nevermind"

Ellie: "You jerk, don't do that to me, finish the sentence, now I'm curious."

Graye: "Don't worry, it's not important."

Ellie: "Fine," *I lean my head back laying flat on the ground*

Ellie: "Whatever" *I sigh closing my eyes as the trees leaves softly scrape against my skin cold air rushing through me*

I feel happy for some reason carefree. Life is better without my parents. Without stress and frustration. The feeling of fear. The world is bright without it. I see why people are scared to get older or to die or not enjoy life to the fullest. I feel so comfortable with Graye that I've never felt like I'm in a dream

< Another Perspective >

a whole another universe if so I would love to like in this lucid dream forever. Too bad everything vanishes.

I slowly open my eyes as clouds overlap, the sun slowly turns to dusk

I quickly turn to the left checking if Graye's still beside me

Ellie: "What time is it?"

he pulls out his phone to check the time

I would check the time on my phone, but he would probably think i'm broke to have a flip phone. You know what. He doesn't seem to mind. Fuck it.

Ellie: "Actually it's fine I realized I brought my phone with me. I'll check the time."

I pull out my flip to check the time hoping he wouldn't judge me

6:10 p.m

Ellie: "It's 6:10."

Graye: "Wow, time went by fast, I can walk you to your house if you'd like."

Time really does fly by when you enjoy the moment. Does he feel mutual with me?

he puts his hands in his front pocket only leaving his thumb out

Ellie: "Would it be bothersome?"

Graye: "No it's fine. I have time at my dad's at work anyways so no one will be waiting for me at home."

I remember when I went to Grayes house since we were partners in a science project 2 years ago. I saw his dad there and many other times when he kissed Graye from school as a kid. I never really saw his mom, but I hesitated to ask.

we slowly walk toward my house not more than 5 inches away from Grayes shoulder

I turn to the right looking at him

Graye: "You cool?"

I quickly splur the words out

Ellie: "Yeah, totally"

Shit, he probably thinks I'm crazy now. He wouldn't be wrong to think that.

we reach a few blocks close to my house

I stopped walking as my curiosity started to bother me

I Know his dad is an alcoholic. It was the subject of the whole block a few years back. What about his mom? I hope this isn't a soft subject to touch on.

Ellie: "Graye...I can talk to you about anything right?"

Graye: "Yeah, no matter what."

Ellie: "Sorry if this question is too personal to answer, but... what happened to your mom?" Okay. I made that sound weird.

< Another Perspective >

Graye: "Oh she's just working, she works a lot that's why you never get to see her."

Ellie: "Really?!"

I guess I overthinked the situation.

Graye: "No I'm playing. I just wanted to see your reaction. Truth is, my parents were always struggling to take care of me and at the time, I was little and dense, thinking that everything was fine. My dad was so humble and kind, but the stress got to him and so he became an alcoholic and workaholic, my mom on the other hand, got into a car accident with nothing else to do."

I shouldn't have asked.

I am stunned from what he just said, but not awed

Graye: "Don't regret asking that question. It's fine I don't mind. I've healed since three years have passed."

It's like he could read my mind. 3 years ago though? That means his mom died one year before I met him.

Graye: "Don't regret anything Ellie. I guess you should know the problem since you are my cure. I passed on...because of you Ellie. You don't know how grateful I am for you.."

Because of me? What have I ever done to help him out in moments of struggle. He shouldn't be thanking me.

a pile of leaves pass by as the wind carries it swooshing away

Graye: "It's getting colder.."

49

he smoothly take out his leather jacket placing it around my shoulder

Graye: "Keep it, you don't want to get sick."

Ellie: "Are you sure? I'll give it to you first thing on monday-"

Graye: "No, I'm fine keep it, you look good in leather jackets."

I smile

Graye: "and you look beautiful when you smile on your own."

Ellie: "Thanks Graye. I can walk from here. You should go home too. I'd feel guilty if you became sick."

Graye: "Okay. Get home safely."

Ellie: "I will, thanks."

he says in a soothing voice as he softly gives a slight wave

we both split off taking the opposite direction

Ellie: "Graye!"

Graye turns halfway in his steps out of curiosity

Ellie: "...Monday 4 p.m, Yoshinoya,....I owe it to a friend."

*He gives the most joyful smile i've seen and salutes with fingers to his head as a goodbye"

Graye: "Until then."

*by now the sun has vanished and it is now pitch black with

< Another Perspective >

a few stars gazing dimly reflecting from my face, the weather gets colder and colder as time passes by*

my mom pulls over the curb suddenly

Aurora: "Ellie, It must have been cold for you to walk home. I was trying to pick you up, but I got carried away, and the time-"

Ellie: "It's fine, I was just finishing up things 'till just now."

Aurora: "Who was that boy just now,"

I hate when she gets into my personal life, but it's better than her yelling at me, at least she's more civilized in this way.

Ellie: "Just a friend, you can say"

Aurora: "Wow, he's handsome, didn't know you even knew people like him."

People like him. That's right, people that are sexy and popular and kind. Unlike you. People like him. No, Grayes different. He's not like them. I myself don't even know why he's hanging out with me.

Aurora: "I suppose he gave you that jacket."

Ellie: "Um yeah, since it was cold."

Aurora: "Why do I only see you hanging out with a guy what a hoe."

Did she think I wouldn't hear that last part, but thanks for the comment anyways.

Aurora: "Wow sweetie look, it's raining massively glad it's a friday so you get to stay home in the heat being cozy."

I can see for myself you know. You don't need to state the obvious. Don't call me sweetie and when was that house ever warm or cozy it's so scary and not the slightest bit heartwarming. You can say it's the best example for a "Home Sweet Home".

she turns on the radio to see the weather for the next following days

Radio: "Broadcasting live from NOAA headquarters. It's raining cats and dogs due to those national typhoons as most of you would like to know about upcoming weather forecasts for California It will be 16% humidity and 90% precipitation as for Saturday April 21, 2018-"

Aurora: "Wow, that's good news though, this place needs rain."

I try grasping onto the idea of something I have forgotten Today is Friday April 20. Time went slow this month.

Ellie: "Saturday April 21, 2018, tomorrow."

I say out the date slowly trying to remember something

Ellie: "Wait...Didn't dad say the funeral was April 22, ?"

Aurora: "Oh my gosh, I forgot all about the funeral, why is it so late after his death date, it's been months, they must have paid a lot for embalming chemicals."

she stops at the red light cessationing her as she reaches out to her purse grabbing her phone handing it to me

Aurora: "Can you put that as a reminder on my calendar Just

< Another Perspective >

In case set my alarm on that day for seven a.m since it starts at eight thirty. I still don't understand why they appointed it so early."

Ellie: "Sure"

I take her phone as she rests her elbow on her left door pressing onto the pedal as the light is now green

I power her phone and go to her calendar app filling april 22nd's spot full; listing "Funeral" When will I ever get a phone like this? That cheap phone isn't good for much.

Aurora: "So did you mark the event on the calendar and set the alarm?"

Ellie: "Yeah, I did."

we reach the garage as I go to my room finished my homework and drew for as long as I felt trying to ignore many things on my mind as It rained for the past two days it was now Sunday; getting ready for the funeral

all ready; I go downstairs

Aurora: "Are you really going to go looking like that?"

she looks at me with a disgusted face

Ellie: "Umm, yeah."

Aurora: "Don't speak to me that way. Say either yes or no and be civilized. Christian's don't dress this way. Maybe It's your attitude and not clothes you need to change."

Ellie: *I mumble* "Maybe you can just shut the fuck up. Maybe if

53

you weren't a fat ass 41 year old woman who gave birth without thinking and wasn't a bitch, things would be better, maybe if you stopped taking things for granted and actually cherished it life would be better, but we can't determine things with maybe or what if."

I never knew there was a dress code for christians and since you always talk on behalf of me can I at least express myself with clothes. What a great way to start the day, not even a "Good Morning". Not like I care.

Navigator: "Turn left onto - street"

Silas: "It's hard to see out here since the fog is covering my view."

Aurora: "We should have taken my car instead of yours. This car is small." No one wants to go in this bitches car. That shit raggedy.

Silas: "My car may be small, but it's quicker than that junk."

Aurora: "Then buy me a new one!"

Silas: "I'm sorry; aren't I poor?"

Aurora: "You're the man, shouldn't you be the one to provide for the family."

Silas: "Stop making excuses, If you want something then work for it." *he grinds his teeth*

Aurora: "That's not what I'm saying-"

Silas: "Just be quiet. You never understand me! I work so hard for a whining wife and mediocre child. You guys can't do

< Another Perspective >

anything! I do so much! You will appreciate this one day! How do you live like this! Disgusting."

I'm just sitting here calmly. They fight for the dumbest reasons and when they lose it they point to others.

Veeram

Vum

Vrer

the windscreen wiper brushed against the wet car front mirror the noise covers the awkward silence

*I opened my book *

Aurora: "Why'd they hold the funeral so far from the main city/"

Silas: "I believe they had plans on moving here before Talon's brother Isaac died."

Aurora: "Oh, they probably wanted the funeral close to the place there moving, but still why would they have an outdoor funeral when the weather's been crazy lately."

I'm surprised they're not arguing like they usually do.

Silas: "I just don't get why someone would kill himself. As I've said I didn't know Isac that well so I can't say if he was Christian or not, but I'm surtian his family was. The family must be embarrassed."

I don't understand how this monster thinks, he stupid. It just doesn't make any fucken' sense. I can't even think in his perspective, maybe that's how he feels about Isaac dying. He couldn't understand Isacs' perspective idea of why he would die, but still!

Ellie: "Isaac must have been suffering enough to lose his own life he probably did believe in God, but maybe the more he suffered he drifted apart from God himself."

awkward silence

Aurora: "Well if he was a true christian or even tried to be he would have held on and believe it would get better by faith in God's power."

Ellie: *mumbles* "There's no point in believing it will get better when it really won't."

Aurora: "Yes! Jesus holds the future. You don't know what will happen next only God knows."

That's just false Hope. Besides, you shouldn't be talking, you're not much of a True Christian yourself as you say.

Silas: "Stop fighting you guys aggravate me. No one cares about your opinion anyways so just sit still until we get to the funeral."

my dad turns up the radio as the silence breaks while we play a Christian playlist

I tilt my head touching my arm resting my elbow on the window

I get quick glimpses of the road as everything passes by

Skrrt

dad hauls the car to a stop

Aurora: "Finally...we're here!"

< Another Perspective >

I get out of the car stretching my sore body from the long ride

*we step into the damp grass to the outdoor funeral and start to walk into the funeral mortuary parlor.

not even seconds later people I couldn't even recognize bombarded us with sorrow hugs

my parents leaving me to talk to others

mom hugs everyone with sympathy as dad hugs others

How fake; she acts like she cares about this funeral, but she could plaster a smile like it's nothing. We seem like we're the perfect ideal family. I can't lie though. Funerals are awkward.

a lady with carrying a metallic tray plate filled with sandwiches approached us Server: "Good Morning." *she tilts her head with a slight smile*

Silas: "Good Morning Ma'am."

Server: "Would you guys like some free sandwiches to start the day."

Silas: "No, thank you."

Aurora: "No, we're fine."

the server turns her neck to look at me Server: "What about you sweetheart."

I give of a sweet expression

Ellie: "Oh thanks, I-"

57

"Mother": "Oh, no. She's fine, we already ate."

I hate it when she does that. When adult's cut me off like they know what I want. How annoying. Don't speak for me.

*though I couldn't recognize most people that surrounded me there was that one that stuck out;

out of them all*

as I'm already annoyed I still think while walking

Why do adults never really care about what the child thinks or wants, but even when they do another adult responds on behalf of me. How would they like it? She wasn't even talking to them. She asked me not my parents just because they don't want doesn't mean I feel the same.

Diem: "Hey~ It's been a while."

Damn. I don't know what I was thinking. Talon's daughter, Isaac's niece of course this bitch would be here. How could I forget?

Diem: "You don't look so good...your face.." *she looks up and down at me* "...and your clothes..." *she cringes to look at me*

Ellie: "I mean, it's a funeral what do you expect. You actually look happy your uncle died though he helped you when times were rough."

Diem: "If only we were friends, I would have given you and your family at least half of Isaac's life insurance money."

Ellie: "Why, so I would be friends just for money that I wouldn't

< Another Perspective >

mind you dragging me like a doll. Nah, I'm fine. Keep your filthy money. I don't need shit from you."

Diem: "Watch that language. Does your parent's know you cuss? How fake of you."

Ellie: "You and you high ass ego."

Diem: "Maybe in your eyes…. I know I'm not perfect. What about you? You sound as if you're always right."

Ellie: "Maybe in your eyes…but have you ever thought maybe I am at least right when we argue because you make bullshit knowing that you're wrong, you just don't want to accept it.

This bitch was jealous of me ever since. Why did dad have to introduce me to her? I should have turned away and ignored acting like I didn't hear her. No, she would try to make me notice her no matter what. I thought she loved her uncle though she always talked about him. Isaac was always kind when it came to Keyona, but she acts like it's her birthday party.

Diem: *rolls her eyes* "I don't even know why I'm talking to you, you're not worth my time, now that I think about it, what was your name again? Sorry I think I have amnesia."

Ellie: "It's Ellie to you."

Diem: "Really for some reason I thought it was a slave."

she covers her mouth as she giggles

I close my eyes Breath Ellie. Just relax

I slowly re-open my eyes

59

Ellie: "Damn. You must really have Amnesia, last time I remembered, just to make it clear I don't like you."

Diem: "Ha! Just to make it clear I don't like you either... actually I hate you, I despise you. You're nothing.

she grits her teeth

Diem: "So, stop acting like you are something."

I wanted to say something back, but I must have been to scared as all I could do was stay still letting her take the last word

she flips her hair as she walks away to her friends at the funeral

What the hell. Why didn't I say anything back. Fuck. Now it seems like I'm scared of her. Maybe I am the only person I knew that wasn't from school or related to me. Guess I didn't know her well enough to stop us from drifting apart.

It starts to sprinkle

laughing

I look up seeing Diem and her friends running indoors from the rain Now I'm all alone. As usual.

< Green Pastures >

Ellie: "Gosh, What should I wear? It's still pretty cold nowadays. I'll stick to pants. I've been thinking since before school started and even after it ended I'm still nervous."

I look at the time near my bed stand

Ellie: "40 Minutes better decide now." *I mumble* "I'm just overthinking, Graye's too sweet. He didn't even say anything about my flip phone and forget about what I wear."

Vrrrr

I look at my desk stand staring at the time, my phone vibrating

Ellie: "Hello."

Aurora: "Hey, I'm going to be working a few hours extra, It's crazy over here. There's some food left on the table for you and Dad, He'll probably be busy at work to eat without us and sleep."

Ellie: "Okay. See you tomorrow then."

Aurora: "Alright, Bye"

She hangs up first, I put my phone in my jacket pocket

Ellie: "Should I wear makeup? Forget it, I'm walking. I should be there early and don't want him thinking I stood him up."

I leave through the front door adjusting my hair Hope I'm decent looking.

Graye: "After you."

I mouth the words Thank you and enter the building

Ellie: "Can't believe you came before me, sorry. How informal of me to invite someone and be second to come."

Graye: "It's fine. I didn't want to be late so I rushed my way here. Guess we both overthink things. *He smiles* "Don't beat yourself over it. Besides, I'm glad I get to spend some time alone with you other than at school."

I'd hate to make him feel dragged to uncomfort. He slightly tilts his head and asks

Graye: "You seem really cold, you alright?"

Ellie: "Oh yeah I just tend to shake a lot when I'm nervous. Anxiety and overthinking gets the best of me."

Graye: "No need to be nervous, I'd be nice to know you better. I feel like you rarely speak your part in conversations. It's Ava, Lucinda, or I leading the dialogue."

Graye: "So, why this place?"

Ellie: "It's one of my favorite places to eat."

< Another Perspective >

Graye looks surprised

Ellie: "Yeah, I'm quite the fat ass."

Graye: "Hahah, Didn't know you cussed or like places such as this."

Ellie: "Guess you were right on not knowing much about me."

Graye: "Aren't I always right?"

we sit in an open table Graye right across from me

I ordered first and graye follow with-

Graye: "Wanna share the food."

Ellie: "Um yeah sure, If you're up for it."

He takes a few bites as I just pick at the chicken

Fuck Ellie. Say something, don't let anxiety get the best of you.

Ellie: "So ho-"

He flicks a piece of food at me

Graye: *He smiles* "Lost your appetite?"

Ellie: ",because I have to see your face while eating."

I throw a bigger portion of food at him

we smile at the same time

Graye: "Wasting money by throwing rice at me. Great choice."

Ellie: "Ha, Bastard you started it first besides I'll waste my money however I want. *I grin*

Graye: "Your money?"

Ellie: "Uhh yeah!"

Graye: "Who said you were paying, as the gentleman we all know we're the ones who pay."

Ellie: "I'm the one who invited you."

he takes a bit of chicken

Graye: "So."

Ellie: "Fine. Go ahead, the pleasure is mine, but if you think you're getting something out of this you're wrong."

Graye: "Wrong? Like I said earlier, aren't I always right?"

Ellie: "You're so annoying," I couldn't stop smiling "I'll pay you back sometime around." I say flushed

Graye: "If it relieves you from feeling in debt then do so, but I'll have you know. I'm quite the fat ass myself."

Ellie: "Fine." *I take a bite of the chicken*

He's so chill. Everything just flows smoothly with him. I was worrying for nothing. He's so nice. Wish things could stay like this.

We soon finish the food, He pays it off like he said we then leave the building

< Another Perspective >

Graye: "You got a ride home?"

Ellie: "Yeah, my legs."

It becomes silent for a few seconds

Graye: "That's another way to say you're walking home."

Ellie: "Hah, took you a moment to realize what I meant to someone pretty slow."

Graye: "Shut Up, Haha!"

we intake the moment

Graye: "If you don't have a specific time to get home, Mind sitting with me."

He nudges his head to a bench Ellie: "Sure, Sounds lovely."

we sit on the bench while the wind blows leaves across grass

Graye: "I still want to know you. I just don't know where to start."

Ellie: "Out of all the things you want to ask me say the first thing out of your mind."

Graye: "You're pretty sad. We'll at least seem like it a lot of times in life. Why do you look so sad in life."

Ellie: "Ha," *I sadly scoff* "Now I don't know where to start."

Graye: "Think about it, and say the first thing you think of."

Ellie: "In general...Everything sucks. Everything just sucks."

65

Graye: "Why?"

Ellie: "I don-" *I take a deep breath* "I don't know why Graye. That's just the world I was given with or maybe it's just me. Sometimes when you're in a field of crazy people and you're the only normal person within that field. You'll soon think you're the crazy person. People think the bigger number tells the truth. Everyone thinks adult's know what's best. That if something bad happened the bigger number will tell the truth compared to the solo person. That's just how shitty my world works for me."

the wind howls He's speechless.

Graye: "Sorry."

Ellie: "For what?"

Graye: "I'm failing as a friend." *He pushes his hair back*

Ellie: "Don't be sorry. You can't just make me happy. No help would make me happy, counseling, talking to someone, I just need my situation to be normal, besides I used to have a "friend" who's a bitch now she should apologize compared to you."

he looks curious

Graye: "Guess that's my next question. What's with that person? Spill the tea."

Ellie: "She was my first friend …..was. We met while both of our parents were hanging out together. Unlike any of my parents' friends ' children. We got along. We were often hyped and would race a lot as fun. Not anymore with my fat self"

we both smirk and slip a laugh

< Another Perspective >

"We both loved to draw and run. I would always bet her at it though, but it's not like I boasted those skills or what not. She then met some new friends from her school that would come to her house when I was also there." *I pause*

"Then she started drifting from me and before I knew it that whole group including her became mean to me. Not like I was their friend. I was only her friend. Now you know typical sad shit she never really told me why she left me, but I guess she was jealous otherwise I don't know what it would be...I don't hate her though."

Graye: "Aww, How nice."

Ellie: "More foolish."

Graye: "You're just sweet that's all."

Ellie: "Wish I wasn't it'll be taken for weakness, It's just hard to forget someone who's given you so much to remember."

we take in the conversation

Graye: "It's alright, you wake up everyday with a new start just keep working at it and mold it into what you want."

Ellie: "Graye, If only things would be like that. Waking up isn't exactly the beginning of something new for me, it's just a continuation. Think of it as the next chapter of a book. My life's so fuck I can't change it at all. It's not even my life. I have no control over it and I'm scared to take control of it. Until I'm 18. When I can leave my parents, fake people and finally...be able to start a new book, but how long can a miserable girl wait in this situation, will I make it be in this situation for 4 more years each millisecond feels so long. I may not make it. Besides how am I so sure that even when I'm 18 life will be better. What if it's the same s*it over and over...or even worse. I'm trapped and I feel so sophisticated. Graye. I hate this place,"

I breath in so heavily

Ellie: "I hate this place so-so much."

Graye: "You can make it. I'm sure of it. I don't know what to do, but If it makes you feel better as soon as you're 18 we can move out of this place to somewhere that can make you feel comfortable and at home."

We? Is he thinking of living with me one day? I might be dead before I see that day come true. Ellie: "If I could even feel those things. Graye....When I say "Place" I mean this whole world." Graye: "How are you so sure of the other side of this world being the same as this world."

Ellie: "You're right on that, but I'm so used to being so sad. Being Happy or even "Normal" to you guys, It just isn't my thing. I'll feel out of place."

he puts his left arm around me touching my left shoulder moving it closer to him

Graye: "Well work on that. Slowly on a slope so soon that you'll see why most people lust for life."

Finding the reason for life. I'll be dead before then.

the wind dances beside us

Graye: "It's the end of April yet it's feeling like the end of November. Are you sure you're able to walk home? I'll accompany you."

< Another Perspective >

Ellie: "Don't need to flex on those manners."

we chuckle

Ellie: "You're probably the only person that laughs this much at my cringe jokes."

Graye: "There you go again with your anxiety and low self esteem."

The wind dances in between inches apart I am from graye

Graye: "Ellie at least let me walk you home so my heart can be assured."

Ellie: "Okay yeah, don't mind your company."

Graye gets up and slowly brushes his hair

Ellie: "Thanks, for being my companion when I'm a summer bummer. What made you want to be friends with Ava, Lucinda and I?" My curiosity peaks.

I may be known as popular to you. Though If it weren't for you guys I'd still be lonely. We smile heartedly.

< Stuck with me >

Graye: "Aye Ellie, You Coming?"

Ellie: "yeah," *I take steps toward him as we sync our steps to the same pace*

Graye: "I can't believe I was almost about to accept you walking home in this weather, sorry if I worry too much that's just me."

Ellie: "Sorry If I look sad a lot of the time, that's just me."

Graye: "Please Ellie, Don't say that."

I can't help it. I know it gets him down a bit knowing I'm sad, but I've bottled this for too long. Someone actually is open to me, I can't help but spew all this burden. I just wish I could be truly happy around him so I can make him have the happiest memories. I feel like the one person I love is getting infected by this. My mental illness is drowning his happiness.

Ellie: "Sorry," *I quickly change the subject*

Ellie: "I actually love the cold.....rather than the heat"

Graye: "Really?! I love the summer, pools, best time for watermelons, natural tanning…"

he rants on and on off the reasons why he loves the summer

Graye: ",and of course, let's not forget girls in bikinis"

Ellie: "As for me, I have a strong Immune system unlike some so I like seeing the people I don't like sick and suffering."

we both laugh

Ellie: "In elementary, remember when I did varieties of activities filling up my time. You kept asking how I had time to do homework and when I said That I didn't even like those activities, but I did them anyway just to not go home."

Graye: "Yeah, I was really shocked at how anyone would stay at school for activities."

Ellie: "Any shitty activity is better than home with them. Summer though. Home with them for around 2 months, God it's dreadful."

Graye: "Thinking about it now, you say "sorry" quite a lot."

Ellie: "I guess so."

Graye: "Yeah, you throw those words out of your mouth like it's nothing."

Ellie: "It is nothing, in a way."

Graye: "What? Hell no those types of words are special as for thank you and I love you."

< Another Perspective >

Ellie: "That's true. I guess I'm just used to it, you know throwing special words like it's nothing for me to say those words they've numbed me so It means nothing to me."

Graye: "Sorry."

Ellie: "Woah! I guess it's contagious."

Graye: "Hah, I really mean it though."

I know you do, you're the only one that means it.

Graye: "Ellie, we're here, thanks for everything."

he shifts his body to leave as the wind dances between us

Ellie: "Not like it's hard to beat, this was the best night I've had."

Graye: "Ellie, my dad found a better job, his always been on step toward falling apart and he thinks moving and starting again in a new place with a better job will help, not to forget he'll stop having taunted memories this place hurts him a bit since she died."

He's speaking of his mother. I'd understand from his perspective.

Graye: "We're moving to Torrance."

he catches me off guard

Ellie: "Well ugh. I don't know what to say."

Don't bombard him with questions. He'll be even more sad knowing that I will.

Ellie: "When will you leave."

Graye: "A week from now, everything's set."

Ellie: "I guess I knew something was up. You seemed distant for a while."

Graye: "I planned to tell you a while back, I just didn;t know the best time."

Ellie: "Yeah and a week before you leave is the best timing to tell me."

Graye: "I'm honestly sorry."

Ellie: "It's fine, I'm messing. Does Ava and Lucinda know."

Graye: "Yes."

Ellie: "Too bad I won't be feeling these types of hugs for awhile, It feels like middle school is going by so slowly."

Graye: "Yeah hopefully it'll go fast as I leave."

Ellie: "Hopefully. As long as we keep in touch."

Graye: "No doubt."

his hands unwrap against me

Graye: "Goodnight, Ellie."

Ellie: "Goodnight."

< Awhile's worth >

2 years later

Eat, School, Wake up, Sleep then arguments when I'm awake.

Aurora: "Ellie woke up already. I have to go to work and there might be traffic due to the weather."

Ellie: "That's fine, I was planning on walking to school anyways."

Aurora: "You're already late and it's snowing, there's going to be traffic."

Ellie: "It's fine, I already told my friends to meet up with me, besides I seem like a burden to you."

I lie just to not carry on the conversation

Don't act like you care.

Aurora: "Then, I'll see you tomorrow."

Ellie: "Tomorrow?"

Aurora: "Yeah, I'm going to your aunt ..." *she smirks* "would you like to come?"

Ellie: "No, I'm busy."

I hate when she provokes me. She knows dad would never let me have contact with any relatives from my Mother's side. They're all evil. According to him and supposedly Jesus agrees with him.

Aurora: "Too busy to see your aunt in 7 years?"

Ellie: "Yeah, life's been pretty hectic, you know what I mean."

"Aunt"? Don't call her my aunt. I only call you Mom and dad, dad because that's what I'm used to other than that you guys are nothing like a mom and dad to me. I don't have a family same for your sisters and extended family; I have absolutely no relationship besides blood links just the thought makes me disgusted.

Aurora: "Ha," *she snickers wickedly* "Okay then, do well in school and serve your dad pot roast for the night."

Ellie: "As always, bye."

Aurora: "Bye."

I get ready

I hear mom leave through the garage Don't ever make the same mistake again.

I grab my Obama phone and keys

I open the door to a cold weather blazing with hail and snow

< Another Perspective >

Ellie: *I say quietly* "I guess it does help to yell sometimes."

I walk in the cold hugging myself looking at the ground

the sound of my feet muffled by the snow I watch my footsteps falling into the snow

Lucinda puts her hand over my shoulder

Lucinda: "Hah, I saw you from afar and called your name like 100 times to catch up. Are you still sleepy or what?"

Ellie: "yeah something like that."

Lucinda: "Did you pull an all nighter for the Science test today? Is that why?"

Ellie: "Science Test? Oh Shit!"

Lucinda: "No? You're always that girl studying to achieve A's. What you watchin' hentai instead of studying."

It's not like I have a choice. A's aren't even good enough for that devil. Besides I study to keep my mind busy. That's the best way to avoid my thoughts, but lately that method hasn't been working out. Hentai was a good guess though.

Ellie: "Yeah, you know I can't last the day without watching Yaoi. Anyways, catch me up on the info."

Lucinda: "Ha, You actually thought I did it."

Ellie: "I'm dead."

I'm fuckin' dead. I've completely forgotten and it's a paper written so I can't search the answers from another tab. There's no way I can cheat, it was all spread around the class. Gosh I didn't even get enough sleep. When do I ever think?

Feels forehead

Should I just ditch? No. This will be the third time I've ditched. They'll think something's up. Maybe I can guess.

see's test

Skylar: "You can just copy me."

And act like a dumbass that's not the move.

Ellie: "No thanks."

Ava: "Hey Ellie, What's up."

Ellie: "Not much. Just failed a test and currently failing at life."

Lucinda comes by my side

Lucinda: "Who's crying, Ellie?!"

Ellie: "No. I don't do those types of things for this reason."

Ava: "What do you mean by that?"

Ellie: "It takes a lot to make me cry."

Lucinda: "Well aren't you tough."

Ellie: "I'm going to the restroom."

Ava: "You want us to wait for you?"

< Another Perspective >

Ellie: "No It's fine, go on without me."

Lucinda: "Um, alright then."

I head towards the restroom checking the area

Good no ones here. I just want to be alone right now.

pulls out a cigarette lighting it up

I take a hit at it

I inhale the fumes

I should just kill myself. What's the point of all this?

Skylar: "Who knew you were emo."

What the fuck!

I quickly look up

Ellie: "What the fuck, This is the girls restroom."

So much for trying not to look stupid in front of him.

Skylar: "and this is school, but here you are smoking in a stall. You don't care about failing tests and leaving your friends to smoke, all at the age of 14."

Ellie: "15"

Skylar: "Since when?."

So we're going to hide the fact that he's hanging at the top of a girls stall.

Ellie: "October 3rd."

Skylar: "Damn i'm late what'd you do on your birthday."

Ellie: "Ate cake...pretty much it. How'd you know I was smoking, what if I was actually using the restroom."

Skylar: "I can smell that shit from afar."

Who knew he cussed. Though he was a goody two shoes.

Ava: "Ellie are you almost done!"

I told her not to wait for me.

Skylar: "Incoming. Move over."

he whispers hopping over the stall now two inches apart from me

What the hell is happening.

I hear her approaching

Ellie: "She'll be able to see your shoes." *I whisper*

Skylar crouches on the toilet seat hiding his feet

Skylar: "Better?"

Ellie: "Better."

Ava: "Ew. What's that smell?!" Oh shit.

Skylar suddenly snatches the cigarette taking a hit then flushing it down the toilet Flusshhh

< Another Perspective >

I spray a light perfume I got from my backpack blushing a little

Ava: "Ellie!"

Ellie: "Sorry, I know I'm taking forever."

What's the point of this? I don't have to make all this effort to hide it. Why do I care about her opinion? Why do I care about human opinions?

Ava: "You takin' a shit or what."

Skylar covers his mouth trying not to laugh

Ellie: "No, I'm sending nude pics to your mom."

Skylar: "Ha,"

Skylar slips a small laugh covering his mouth, gripping shut

Ellie: "I'll be there in a sec'."

Ava: "Alright then."

Ellie: "You better not tell anyone about this." *I whisper to Skylar*

he nods

From Aurora and Silas's tool, Skylar's puppy to Elizabeth's ragdoll and now a drug junkie. Damn, what a failure.

I leave the stall washing my hands acting like I was using the restroom, but also by the strong scent the vapor left on my hand

Lucinda grunts as we run

Ellie: "I hate running in the heat, but is it really that bad for you?"

Lucinda: "Hell yeah, I'm dying. You're so lucky you're smart and fast as fuck"

Ellie: "Practice, I truly work for it."

Sooner or later I'll be catching up to your pace. The drugs will get to me and my lungs will soon be corrupted just like my soul.

Lucinda: "You can go ahead without me."

Ellie: "We can make it together. I'm good."

Same thing over and over I'm getting exhausted from life more and more. I guess my body takes after my thoughts. I run away from so many things and as for me I am fast. Does that mean I'll be dead soon? How lovely would that be.

Lucinda: "Really, you're so lucky. I hate running and I wanna die."

Ellie: "You can say that again."

lucinda puts her hands on her knees

Ellie: "Hey, we actually made it in time."

Lucinda: "Hahh, Yeah" *she speaks out of breath*

she gets a sip of water and sits on the concrete cold ground

Lucinda: "Hey have you heard of the party happening in a month."

< Another Perspective >

Ellie: "No... and No." *I bluntly say knowing what she'll say next*

Lucinda: "Come on Ellie, it's an open invite. You'd have so much fun."

Ellie: "No thanks, I'm not into parties, besides who's even hosting it?"

Lucinda: "Not sure someone just spread it via social media now it's the talk of the school."

Ellie: "Is Ava going?"

Lucinda: "Hell yeah you know that girl's a party animal. Come on, it's the ceremony of promoting high school. Think about it."

Ellie: "Fine I'll give it a thought, though I most likely know my final decision." I should probably go anyways to keep her company. We'll see.

Ava and Lucinda enter science class

Mrs.Provence: "Homework?"

Ellie: "Sorry."

She's totally going to get on my head

she clicks her tongue shaking her head

Mrs.Provence: "This is how you bring your grade up. I hope you're not going to that party I've heard about, use that time to make up your assignments. What happened you used to be so good in this class?"

she walks away collecting other students homework

83

Did she want me to answer what happened to me? I'm not going to be any type of doctor. Yeah, Money isn't happiness, but money sure gives me many opportunities to be happy. Just not like that. Will I be stuck in the same boring hospital for days to come working and sleeping until I die. Is there even a chance I'll make it 'till 18?

I feel a slight tap on my shoulder and slowly turn my head

Skylar: "Speaking of parties, you're going right?"

Ellie: "I'm not sure."

Skylar: "What? Don't tell me you're taking her words to heart. You really want to study?"

Ellie: "Whether I study or not. I'm not interested in parties."

Skylar: "Come on, tell me what will make it fun. I'll do it for you."

Ellie: "You know the host well enough?"

Skylar: "It's my party."

Ellie: "Oh, I don't know, I just want some time to think about it."

Skylar: "I get it. You're good though?"

Ellie: "Yeah"

Maybe I'll go not just for Lucinda's sake, but Skylar will be there. Why not... Mrs.Provence: "I hope you're not daydreaming Ellie." *She whispers to me madly*

Ellie: "Even better, I'm talking to my demons." *I whisper back annoyingly joking*

< Another Perspective >

Mrs.Provence: "Very funny, I'm sure they won't help you bring your grade up, might wanna study Ellie."

I hate how she's forcing me to study. They just shove things down your throat. They don't care about us, only for grades, because it reflects on how these people teach. No, these inner thoughts won't give me the answers for science, but they'll help me avoid all of this. If I die. I wouldn't need to raise it. I wouldn't have to care, would I?

Skylar passes a note over my shoulder landing onto my desk

I look back at him as he grins resting his head on his hand, I turn back around quickly grabbing the note shoving it in my backpack filled with rubbish materials

I'll read it later. No rush. Least I won't is having her read it in class.

Ellie: "Oh Gosh. That class feels so dragged out." *I mumble placing my hands on my head*

Ava: "'least it's lunch time."

Lucinda: "Even lunch is ruined with the crappy shit they call nutritional food."

Ellie: "Yeah, you wanna just walk around."

my phone vibrates in my backpack

Ellie: "I'll catch up with you guys in a moment."

Ava: "Alright."

I reach into my backpack seeing the letter I totally forgot about that letter

I answer the phone

Ellie: "Your call is being automated to a message-"

Skylar: "Very funny."

Ellie: "Skylar?"

He sounds very close. Is he breathing into the phone?

I look around Nevermind.

I move my phone from my ear and walk to Skylar

I feel people glancing at me

Skylar: "What's your answer."

Ellie: "I still haven't decided on going to the party."

Skylar: "Not on that, Did you read the letter?"

Ellie: "Not yet, I forgot until I searched for my phone in my backpack."

Skylar: "Did you smoke recently? You seem slower than ever."

Ellie: "Shut up." *I nudge him rolling my eyes smiling*

Skylar: "What are you waiting for."

Ellie: "I don't know I'm anxious, anxiety gets the best of me."

< Another Perspective >

Skylar: "The fuck is their to be scared about, if it's bad it's bad and if it's good it's good." What a rare mindset.

Ellie: "It's not that easy...maybe you can give me a hint...Is it bad?"

Skylar: "Depends.." *he whispers*

my spines shiver

I hate feeling like I'm walking on eggshells around him. I always have to be perfect for my lover. He's nostalgic and scary. Something mesmerizing about him. I don't think it's good though, but I can't help it. As if they were both magnets. I hate and love the feeling. It's never that easy to explain.

Ellie: "I'll open it later."

Skylar: "Fine."

Ellie: "By the way...how'd you get my number."

Skylar: "I asked Ava."

Ellie: "Sure stalker not to mention that bathroom peeking moment."

Skylar: "Seriously though, Did you guys just make up from a fight, I mean I just saw you guys walking together a while ago but,"

Ellie: "What makes you think that."

Skylar: "Maybe it was the part where she seemed distraught when I asked for your number." Maybe it's because she likes you too, she probably hates the idea of us getting closer.

Ellie: "I wonder why."

Skylar: "Nevermind, I might be thinking too much, a hit in the park?"

I look confused for abit

Ellie: "You're asking me to smoke in a park illegally in public?"

Skylar: "We both look older than we are, no one will question. Tomorrow, not today since I'm busy."

Ellie: "What a risk taker."

Ava: "what're you guys talking about?" *she quickly jumps in*

Ellie: "The party….. Skylar's hosting, are you going?"

Ava: "Of course," "especially if he's going" *she whispers to me with a smirk*

Ellie: "Cool" *I say unbothered*

I turn to walk away

Ellie: "Skylar, I'll be going to the party...and park." Gosh, I have a headache.

I smoke on and on shaking my foot

Should I read it? I'm thinking too hard. It's already been 7 hours since he gave this letter to me. I should just get over it. Fuck it. Just do it. Come on now. It's 3:08. Don't drag things out any further.

I reach for it out of my backpack

< Another Perspective >

Maybe I should say I lost it and have him just say it to me. No stop it, just fuckin read it.

I open the crumpled letter

COuGH
  COUgH
    COUGHHH

I can't breathe, I need water.

my eyes quickly scan the room looking for water, I crush the bottle a bit gulping it down

I See light peeking under my door Fuck. She's awake. I'm dead.

I hop over my bed and prop the window open

I hear footsteps coming closer

I motion my hands left and right trying to get the fumes to dilute I'm hella dead. What about the message?

I slither in bed and pretend to be asleep

the door creaks open

Aurora: "Are you asleep? What's that smell?"

Ellie: "Hmmm" *I mumble acting tired*

Aurora: "It smells like herbs. There's probably fungus since you don't clean your room."

What the fuck.....You know what i shouldn't complain, better

89

than her finding out. Why should I hide this though. She cheated. Smoking isn't something she should care about. My room isn't that bad though

Ellie: "Yea, yea, I'll clean it tomorrow. Can I go to sleep so I'm not late for school."

Aurora: "Goodnight."

I hear her step into her bedroom

He loves me, I smile, shake my head, and unbelievably I whisper at night.

< Forgetting those days >

Well he didn't ask me out...He wrote it out.

I roll around my bed as silent as I can

Relax Ellie. What if he's joking and playing with me? Should I act tough or-

Ellie: "Hello"

Ava: "Hey, Sorry if it's too late I figured you'd be getting ready for school by now."

Ellie: "haha" *I fake laugh* "At 3:30 of course I would."

Ava: "I just woke up and suddenly remembered....you saying you were going to the party. I couldn't hear much, but I made out the words."

Ellie: "Yea, I'm going."

Oh gosh, what should I do with Ava. She likes him too. I should ask for her permission. She's my friend after all. How should I start the conversation?

Ava: "Oh shit, for reals! All three of us are going to be matching."
Matching and then what a threesome?

Ellie: "Skylar, you, and I...matching?"

Ava: "What the fuck, no, I meant Lucinda, you, and I."

Ellie: "I'm only joking, I'll be busy trying to maintain my grades -forget raising them-."

Ava: "Alright then-

"Good night" *we say in sync*

Ava: "Or good morning, I should say"

It's like I could hear her smirk through the phone as I hang up

Fuck! What was I thinking Skylar could fit in skinny jeans and match. Gosh, that was embarrassing. I'm tired...I'll save this shit for tomorrow. When should I tell her? Should I just say it casually or bring it up out of a random conversation?

Ellie: "Skylar. He asked me on a date."

Ava: "I'm Sorry?" *she says puzzled*

Ellie: "He wants to go out with me."

Ava: "Hahaheh" *she laughs*

Ava: "Can you believe it, Skylar wants Ellie." Why say it like that?

Ellie: "Yeah?" I give a peculiar tone and bring sharp eye glares

< Another Perspective >

Lucinda: "You guys are dating. Congratulations!"

Ellie: "No. Not really. I didn't say yes. He wrote it on a note."

Lucinda: "Aww on a note that's so cringey yet romantic nostalgia of highschool love."

Ava: "...Prove it."

I hand her the crumpled paper

she snatches it, they quickly read it

Ava: "You probably wrote this yourself."

Lucinda: "Doesn't seem like her handwriting."

Why is it that Ava's trying to prove me wrong? She probably thinks no guy like Skylar would go for me... or she's jealous. I'd hate to be one.

Ellie: "You can ask him."

Lucinda: "Why didn't you say yes though."

Ava: "Why are you telling us so soon also, You want to rub it in our face." *she smiles with a gloomy face*

Should I say it in front of Lucinda. I mean she's chill and knows we both like him.

Ellie: "I mean I liked him from a while back, but it might make you awkward or sad and I don't want you to be in that position from this situation."

Ava: "So you're asking me for permission to date him?"

93

I shrud

Ellie: "Yeah, I guess so."

Ava: "I'm fine with it."

Ellie: "Really?"

Ava: "No, I changed my mind...just kidding."

Ellie: "Oh gosh." *I smile a bit*

Lucinda: "While you're craving for Skylar I'm hungry enough to crave this nasty ass school lunch."

Ava: "Alright, let's head there." *she tilts her head to the direction and smiles* So that's a yes. Woah, kinda didn't think this far out. So what now?

we eat lunch quietly me and ava quickly sharing glances Fuck, it's so awkward.

"Do you guys normally eat together quietly?"

I get startled as Skylar quickly sits next to me Now I'm embarrassed. Gosh, people are staring.

Lucinda: "There's the new couple."

Skylar: "They know?"

Ellie: "Yeah."

Skylar: "So... this is me asking you out officially. You wanna date?"

< Another Perspective >

Ellie: "Yeah?"

Is this really happening? I don't feel so great...

Skylar: "Where would you like to go as a first date?"

Ellie: "I'm fine with anything."

Skylar: "The movie theater...Today at 8?"

Ellie: "Yeah"

It seems like the only agreement word I say is "Yeah".

Ellie: "I mean yes that's fine."

Gosh this again? What should I wear now? Fuck it i'm overthinking.

I put on pants and a sweatshirt Gosh, it's cold. I like it.

Someone bumps my shoulder Damn, rude.

I look straight and almost tramp on Skylar

Skylar: "Woah," *He grabs my shoulder* "You good?"

Ellie: "Yeah, Sorry."

I quickly take his hand off my shoulder

he looks a bit mortified

Ellie: "It's just that people from our school are staring at us."

Skylar: "So? Gosh, that anxiety. We're dating and the whole

95

school will realise eventually." You're such a "popular guy". Of course they will. People can't mind their business.

I wish they wouldn't though.

Skylar: "What type of movies do you like?"

he switches the vibe Ellie: "Horror's my thing."

Skylar: "Aye, I can go with that. I don't really have a preference just not from com....shit makes me gag."

Ellie: "Horror it is."

Skylar: "Do you want food?"

Ellie: "No thanks."

Skylar: "You're not starving yourself are you?"

Ellie: "No I'm not. I just refuse to eat spinach for dinner constantly."

Skylar: "Two tickets please." *he turns to me* "Do you eat healthy all the time?"

Ellie: "Mostly and I get sick of it and spend my money on outside food ever so often."

Skylar: "Thanks." *he grabs the tickets*

Ellie: "I'll pay you back."

Skylar: "Please don't, It won't make me feel like boyfriend material."

< Another Perspective >

Ellie: "Whatever the fuck that means."

Skylar: "Are you always so stubborn yet open minded?"

Ellie: "Fine, thanks for paying."

Skylar: "No problem, least I can do for my girl."

Ellie: "Let's go get our seats."

I say as if I didn't hear what he just said

Skylar: "Yeah, Sure thing."

I'm not really feeling it today.

we sit in the middle center of the theater quietly watching

Skylar: "Did you like the movie?"

Ellie: "Yeah, It was better than I thought."

Skylar: "Is it okay if I talk to my friends, It'll take a few moments."

Ellie: "Feel free." *I look and grin to his friends as a greeting then turn away*

I could feel their glare. Their staring. Quite a few people are. Gosh this is embarrassing. I hate when people stare.

I look at the sky

It's really just been 2 years since Graye left. I feel like the only one still thinking of him. Times so dragged out.

Skylar: "Whatcha' doing?"

97

Ellie: "Star gazing...or something like that."

Skylar: "Sounds boring."

Ellie: "Yeah, I'm boring."

Skylar: "You went from horror and dark jokes to star gazing."

Ellie: "Is this the part where I say 'I'm not like other girls'".

Skylar: "It sounds boring lets see if it really is."

Ellie: "Talk to me...What's your favorite color?"

Skylar: "Haha, Blue and yours?"

we star gaze Ellie: "Black."

Skylar: "Thought you'd say pink."

Ellie: "You must be joking, I hate that color, though I have some outfits with pink that look really good. I told you...I'm not like other girls." *I quickly glance while he stares at the stars*

Ellie: "What made you want to date me."

Skylar: "It was obvious you liked me years back, I toyed with you, then simply decided to date you."

Ellie: "Damn, thought I was good at hiding it hah, that's all. Many other girls like you."

Skylar: "I know."

Ellie: "Then why go for me?"

< Another Perspective >

he looks at me

Skylar: ",because you are not like other girls."

Ellie: "Yeah, I'm worse."

Skylar: "How so?"

I shouldn't tell him yet. We barely started. I don't want to bomb him with my feelings.

Ellie: "I'm playing."

Skylar: "I've heard you have really dark humor from Lucinda."

Ellie: "Yeah it's something we share."

Skylar: "Isn't it known that every joke has some part of truth."
He's right. I say things and quickly say I'm joking to take it back.

Ellie: "That's not the case for me. Jokes are just jokes when I say them."

Skylar: "Thank God, all these emo teens nowadays such a turn off to generations." Ellie: "What do you mean?"

Skylar: "All these kids nowadays are saying they are depressed. It's fucking annoying."

Ellie: "I get that, but some may actually be depressed. Mental illnesses don't really have a specific age to start, and it's a turn off?

Skylar: "Yeah, I can't date no chic being a bummer." I'll be dragging him down

Ellie: "I'm pretty exhausted Skylar, Goodnight." Skylar: "Already?, I love you!"

Ellie: "Wow, horny boy."

Skylar: "I swear it's not like that."

he smiles

It hit me at that moment. We were dating, but I realized things could be so different. I can actually talk to someone when I'm hurt. Even hang out with someone without feeling needy. Be truly happy for once.

Honestly, I lived every day of my childhood in fear. Most of it is gone, the fact that I'm 15 and spent my days so miserably made me so bitterly sad. I'm afraid to be happy, because whenever I do get happy bad shit eventually happens. Others would enjoy the moment making so much out of it filled with happy memories and I would cry the night away accepting that I would die young and alone.

Skyalr comes in to kiss me

Skylar: "The days just started and you look exhausted."

Ellie: "Typical shit keeps me up."

I can make it. As soon as I'm 18, I'll leave these monsters... get to have my own freedom with Skylar. What a wild reality.

Skylar: "Well stop being stressed it's not good."

I fake a smile

Skylar: "I mean try to think positive."

< Another Perspective >

Ellie: "Woah, you care for me, how cute."

Skylar: "Of Course I do, I Love you."

Ellie: "You don't even know me that well." Neither do I, but I've liked him all this time.

Skylar: "Then tell me about yourself."

Ellie: "Well shit, where do I start? It's so much."

Skylar: "Anywhere,"

I'm not really the type to open up first, But I brought this on myself.

Skylar: "Actually save it for tonight, let's have another date."

Ellie: "Already, 2 In a row?"

Skylar: "Why not, Let's meet at my house."

He was fast at things. He knew what he wanted and rushed for it. Normally I'd tell him we have time and should slow the pace, but do we have time.

Ellie: "What about your parents."

Skylar: "What about them, they'll be gone for awhile they won't even be back before the party."

He's so different from others I meet a bit of a bad guy. Maybe I needed this, Life is boring.

Times have been going so slow for all I've known.

Ellie: "Okay."

Skylar: "Mission accomplished. At 8."

I smile

Ellie: "Okay." *I say once more*

Skylar smiles Skylar "Okay."

Ellie: "Don't mock me asshole."

Skylar laughs Skylar: "Okay."

I roll my eyes

Ellie: "I'll see you tonight."

< In Comparison >

Skylar: "Go on now."

Ellie: "I promise you'll be bored."

My anxiety is at its highest peak.

Ellie: "I- I started smoking in 9th grade when I was 14, I hate parties and reunions, but people still manage to drag me to them." *I look at him and smile* "Supposedly I'm a good liar, My favorite color is Black. I love Pizza and Cheeseburgers, but not obesity.

He catches the joke and laughs

Ellie: "I have family issues, schools are so stressful, but it's better than being at home. I-"

Skylar: "Weren't you smart?"

Ellie: "Elaborate please."

Skylar: "You were smart and fast as far as I knew. I thought HighSchool would be nothing for you. The only person who had a chance into an Ivy League University as a matter of fact."

Ellie: "I came to realization."

Skylar: "..Of what?"

Ellie: "Life isn't that great for me."

He suspects that I'm being abused, I don't even know that for sure. Skylar: "For example."

Ellie: "I know what you're trying to confirm and I won't tell you."

Skylar: "If you are, just tell me."

That's the opposite of what I just said. Ellie: "...Then what."

Skylar: "We can see." That's not quite assuring.

Skylar: "Just be honest, that's all I'm asking."

For a girl that has lots of secrets. That's way too much to ask for. Ellie: "Fuck. I'm quite speechless."

Skylar: "Just tell me honestly, Please."

Ellie: "They're just really strict that's all. Nothing else to it."

Skylar: "That's a lie. Come on."

Ellie: "It's really not."

Skylar: "What made you hesitate to say they're just strict then."

Ellie: "I don't know what to say."

Skylar: "Just speak what's real."

< Another Perspective >

Ellie: "What's real nowadays... you seem like you know what's the answer."

Skylar: "Yeah pretty much."

Ellie: "Then why are you asking this question."

Skylar: "I want you to say it."

That I feel trapped by my so-called family.

Ellie: *sigh* "Tell me about yourself."

Skylar: "I smoke for fun, social drinker, party animal, best host in this town may I add that."

Ellie: "Ha, I know, I know, I'll go."

Skylar: "Your strict parents will let you?"

Ellie: "Hell no, I can't hang with a dude without my mom thinking I'm a slut."

Skylar: "You're going to sneak out?"

Ellie: "Yeah."

Skylar: "Why are your parents so strict."

Ellie: "They overthink everything and think so many things are a sin. I honestly feel caged. Some may think they just want the best, but no. When you're this strict you just teach me to lie, rebel." They interpret the Bible to another level. People testify on how saved and re-born they feel when becoming religious. Yet, Religion drifted us apart."

Skylar: "Imagine if your parents found out you did drugs and even though you try you can't get all As."

Ellie: "Yeah, Imagine when my parents find me dead."

Skylar: "...They'll be devastated."

Ellie: "Of Course, because their reputation will be ruined. Everyone will know that the most perfect holy family telling others that God will save you, couldn't even save their own daughter."

Skylar: "This is a constant saying, but killing yourself spreads the pain to others. You only have one life anyways"

Ellie: "Good. Not one of them loves me. They take all that shit for granted. I never asked for this life and I certainly don't want it. So good. I hope every single one of them feel the pain and guilt forever let them contemplate how the fuck they treated me. Honestly though...they probably will think of things for a moment but I know after a while things will die down and they'll forget everything. Such ignorant people."

Skylar: "Damn, Talk to a counselor or some shit."

Ellie: "Why would I risk that. What if I tell them? They'll investigate the house quickly to be greeted by a hypocritical fake ass family that will deny everything. Then as soon as they leave I'll be having my consequences by them. Skylar I've thought of many things. Even running away, but then after I steal whatever amount from them how long I can last."

Skylar: "Just live off of Cup o Noodles."

Ellie: "Then I'll die from high sodium rather than starvation."

< Another Perspective >

We give a sad memorable laugh

Skylar: "No escaping. Now I'm speechless."

Ellie: "It's fine. I'll take advantage of living under their roof until I'm 18. Then I'll leave wherever I planned and never see these bitches again."

Skylar: "You going to a University?"

Ellie: "Honestly I have to be a cardiologist so yeah, College is the gate way for me to be free though. I'll live in adorm get my shit together to save money from a part time Job until I have enough to never see my parents again."

Skylar: "Then stop slacking."

Ellie: "I don't know. Maybe I should just be a slutty stripper."

Skylar: "Let's see what your parents have to say about that."

Ellie: "What's up with your fam?"

Skylar: "Nothing juicy. My dad being bossy just orders my mom around and life goes on."

Ellie: "Orders her to do what."

Skylar: "Simple chores."

Ellie: "Seems like a slave that's harsh."

Skylar: "No he's kind of an asshole, but she doesn't mind. It doesn't seem like she does. Who's worse, Your mom or Dad?"

Ellie: "Gosh they both uniquely shit in their own way. My mom is annoying and, my dad, well he scares me. They both share narrow visions and they are a horrible married couple using the excuse that they haven't divorced for my sake supposedly."

Skylar: "Do you want them too?"

Ellie: "It's shit honestly. They argue for the dumbest shit for so long and they both always think their right and have such high ego, neither one of them apologises. They just wait till it dies down, ignore each other vent about each other to me, and I'm just so tired. It would be for the best in my opinion, their hella toxic. It wasn't meant to be."

Skylar: "Yeah.....Yeah I get that."

Ellie: "Well thank you Skylar, for tonight,-"

Skylar: "Already? Oh shit, yeah it's gonna be late. Hope your strict parents won't get mad, I could drive you."

Ellie: "You have a car? A Permit too?"

Skylar: "Yeah the privilege of a 16 year old. Sucks for you."

Ellie: "I'm fine though."

He leads me out the door

Skylar: "Tell me where your crib is."

he ignores my stubbornness Ellie: "Okay, fine."

Even if he didn't understand I wouldn't care. He listened.

we drive around the common block as I direct him Ellie:

< Another Perspective >

"Imagine if we had more nights like this." Instead I spend the night alone in despair.

Skylar: "Why not."

Ellie: "My parents will get suspicious and mad and make some dumb ass reason to be, eventually we will though, when i'm 18."

Skylar: "You really want to be 18 huh?"

Ellie: "I guess that's not the same for you?"

Skylar: "I never want to be 18."

Ellie: "really?"

Skylar: "Yeah, It's scary getting old. Bills, more responsibility, death, don't forget the wrinkles."

Ellie: "I'd pay the price to all of that to be happy."

Skylar: "Will you really be?"

Ellie: "Be happy?"

Skylar: "You are not a minor anymore, cardiologist, you prove others wrong, haven't seen or talked to your fam in years, that's your plan right?"

Ellie: "Yeah."

Skylar: ",and you'll be happy?"

Ellie: "Yeah."

Skylar: "Say something other than 'yeah'."

Ellie: "...I'll be happy Skylar."

Skylar: "You sure."

Ellie: "Haha and if not oh well."

Skylar: "Oh well?"

Ellie: "That's my plan in life, Not happy? Oh well.."

Skylar: "Sounds like a mission not a plan in life."

Ellie: "Like you've said...well see."

I open the door stepping out Skylar: "Goodnight."

I shut the door

Skylar: "Damn Just like that!"

he smiles

Ellie: "You shouldn't say 'I love you' to expect the same back."

I mock in a squeaky voice Ellie: "Goodnight sweetheart."

< Summer Soirée >

Skylar: "So, is this indefinite?"

Ellie: "I usually get back by 4 in the morning."

Skylar: "You're really sneaking out. You're such a bad person." *He jokes* "It'll be worth it. I promise."

Ellie: "Have you talked to Ava and Lucinda?"

Skylar: "They're already on their way."

Ellie: "What was Ava's tone."

Skylar: "um normal as usual, bring a swimsuit."

Ellie: "I don't plan on swimming."

Skylar: "You weren't planning on coming to my party. Look what you're getting ready for now though."

Ellie: "I'll be more stubborn this time. I won't swim, I'm sure of it."

Skylar: "Party bummer."

Ellie: "Too bad, see you soon."

Skylar: "Love you."

Ellie: "Same here."

The cringe of highschool lovers. The types that never last.

I slip out the kitchen window and hope the fence

I constantly check my phone glaring bright lights into the darkened night until I face Skylar's house filled with people and glowing lights

Skylar: "Bout time! Want a drink?"

he tires to hand me one Ellie: "No thanks."

Skylar: "What, why not? Oh you don't want your friends to know about it. Why? Who gives a fuck what they think"

Ellie: "Me. I care, and you can't lie that you care too. At least a little bit."

Skylar: "Just a little, but not to the point where I have anxiety."

Ellie: "I wanna keep my streak."

Skylar: "Wow, you're staying sober, look at you making big moves."

we walk to the pool and sit on the side with music echoing

Ellie: "Remember when we were little kids eating boli popsicles. Now we're doing drugs and alcohol."

< Another Perspective >

Skylar: "'when we were little' We're not that old just yet, you know?"

Ellie: "Time feels so slow, but we're moving too fast for our age."

Skylar: "especially you."

Ellie: "Me?"

Skylar: "Parties and drugs are something, but you want to die and you're just 15."

Ellie: "Yeah, I know, and I don't care."

Skylar: "Damn, you're just going to give up?"

Ellie: "I'm not 'giving up' shit, this was never mine to begin with. It doesn't matter anymore."

Skylar: ",but it did before?"

Ellie: "Back when I was innocent. Fuck it though."

Skylar: "You're gonna just leave me like that."

Ellie: "Oh shit I forgot. I'm joking."

he just stares at me with a small smile Skylar: "Dance?"

Ellie: "No, I'm fine."

Skylar: "Come on, I promised a good party, but you're not helping. At Least dance, I can teach you if that's the problem."

Ellie: "Okay I'll dance. I got it, just not to do something slow."

he leaves his drink and pulls my hand leading to his living room Shit, it's packed.

the next song starts

I think people are now us now. They're just staring.

Skylar: "Shit, for some reason these ones slow."

Ellie: "Skylar, do something your the host, cunt."

I see what he's doing.

Skylar: "Hah, It's time you do something without anxiety holding you."

Ellie: "Gosh okay."

he puts his arm around my waist

Ellie: "Shit like this is cringey to me that's why."

he leads my hands to his shoulder Skylar: "Are you enjoying it?"

Ellie: "Yeah I guess, Skylar, Thanks."

Skylar: "For this party? It's nothing I have the mon-"

Ellie: "For listening to my issues, I've done it many times. Listening to others. I never was the talker."

Skylar: "No problem."

Ellie: "There's your one and only dance with me, go be a good host, I'll hang with Ava and Lucinda."

< Another Perspective >

Skylar: "I'm a good one without even trying."

we part ways as I spot lucinda

Ellie: "You like parties? You seem to enjoy it a lot."

Lucinda: "You're so isolated, parties are awesome. One day I'll throw my own, bigger than Gatsby's."

Ellie: "Aha, Where's Ava?"

Lucinda: "She wanted 'fresh air'.She can never take second hand smoke."

Ellie: "oh okay."

Lucinda: "Don't worry, why don't you hit the pool."

Ellie: "Not feeling it, and You?"

Lucinda: "Can't swim remember, I'll just stick to the dance floor."

I wonder if Graye is enjoying the summer. Watching hot girls in bathing suits while he swims.

I smile thinking of him Lucinda: "What's so funny?"

Ellie: "Do you remember Graye?"

Lucinda: "yeah of course. It's been awhile."

Ellie: "It feels longer than 2 years, do you still chat with him?"

Lucinda: "Occasionally just a 'hey, how are you' every other month."

We're drifting apart, but what can I do?

Ellie: "I'm going to sit for a bit, text me when you're ready to leave."

I slide through people and sit watching Lucinda dance the night from a distance

She's taking a while just for "fresh air". Maybe she's hurt or lost...or getting laid, but that's quite unlikely.

I call her as it goes to voicemail

I stand up and walk to an uncertain destination Might as well look for her. Since she's not picking up.

I search for her and tour myself through Skylar's house She's nowhere to be found.

I think to myself before spotting her between bushes She's so making out. *I smile*

I walk closer and my smile vanishes

I thought she was fine with it. I thought I would be happy. I truly thought he loved me.

I watch skylar and ava go on as if i was paralyzed until I turn around I'm such a dumbass.

I drag my feet to his shelf and pour myself as I drink a cup If I can't have him might as well enjoy free drinks.

I sit back by the pool and stare away Lucinda: "Did you find her?"

< Another Perspective >

Ellie: "Yeah" *I say continuing to stare at the pool* Lucinda: "Where at?"

I sit in silence Lucinda: "Ellie?" "Is she high?"

A guy Lucinda danced with asks Lucinda: "We don't smoke."

I do.

I stop lagging and respond quietly Ellie: "Some bushes around the back."

I always disliked summer but this year was the cherry on top to the reasons why.

Lucinda figures I don't want to talk and leaves me

I stared at nothing for a good few seconds, and In those seconds I observed in silence. Didn't want to stay, Didn't want to leave. I was stuck, Trapped. This time it wasn't in my house.

I watched it fall apart without the strength to hold or bring it back up. I don't mind if others did it, but I hated to cry. I'd physically confirm my enemies have won if so. They have though, I surrendered long ago. They bash at a dead body and soul. I couldn't help but cry - still observing.

I cuff my pants and dip into the water contemplating on what has went wrong in life

I walk home alone to then sit in the corner of my dim room

You have 3 hours to finish your homework and sleep. That's more important. My fingers drag against my binder and look straight away.

Well see, If i wasn't alive I wouldn't deal with this crap. No homework, Got no deep fear of not being successful. True people to hang with, none of it. My fingers dig to paper

What now?

God, I need new friends.

< So-called friends >

Aurora: "What do you want to do?"

Ellie: "What?"

Aurora: "Your birthday's coming up."

Ellie: "Oh, yeah. I don't really have anything in mind. It's fine."

she puts the cake in the fridge Ellie: "Pineapple upside down."

Aurora: "They didn't have many choices. It was either that or chocolate." I'd take chocolate over this any time.

Ellie: "Hah, they messed up my name too. Must be hard to spell Ellie," *I burst a small laugh* "It's all good, gotta go."

Aurora: "I'll remind your dad so we can celebrate together."

Ellie: "Go ahead. Thanks for the cake anyways."

Haven't felt the slightest bit appreciated in a while. I can't be ditching school, but I don't want to go. What should I say?

Aurora: "Why are you always late."

She's just worried that this will hold me back from being a damn cardiologist.

Ellie: "At least I show up, besides I don't eat breakfast so it's not like I'm tardy, It's not on my record so relax."

Aurora: "Don't talk to me like that."

Ellie: "Like what."

Aurora: "I hear the attitude in your tone."

Ellie: "Honestly, that's just how I sound, but if you don't want me talking that way then don't talk to me at all."

Aurora: "I'm your mother!"

Ellie: "And? Then act like it."

She gets more annoying as time passes. This summer was shit, and school is just as bad nowadays. I hope Graye had a better one than me. Spending his time sunbathing, lurking by the pool while I heard arguments echo the house early in the morning and becoming broken by someone I shared my secret thoughts and feelings with.

Skylar: "Ellie, What happened? We've been spamming you."

Ellie: "I powered it off for a while, been busy."

Skylar: "Busy enough to not text something simple so we know you're fine." But I'm not fine.

Ellie: "Yeah, busier than you were smooching on my friend."

Skylar: "What?"

< Another Perspective >

She wasn't a friend.

Ellie: "Well I'm here now."

How do I start? Should I even say anything? What if I do? He'll leave me.

He reaches for my hand but I move away He was never mine to begin with.

Skylar: "I had plans for the summer with us, but you didn't pick up your phone." I had plans for us for years to come.

I look down to not look at him

I can't continue. He's just like mom. God, why am I surrounded by people who hurt me.

Ellie: "There's an end of the summer festival we can go to tonight."

Our last date.

Skylar: "Oh yeah, never been to it. We can celebrate 6 months in the meantime."

6 months. Yeah, It's been 6 months. It felt longer. I got pretty comfortable. Though it was nothing for him.

Ellie: "Ok bye."

Skylar: "Well wait!"

Skylar: "It's really been half a year." *he hastily hands me items*

Skylar: "Well this is pretty special, Your favorite color is black and I don't know. I just got creative. Well not really- I checked on reddit what girls like. A man's hoodie and necklace came first."

Ellie: "I'm fine."

Skylar: "I'm not really good with relationships so this is a big deal for me."

Ellie: "This was so much more for me, maybe you'd be better with relationships if you were truly committed."

he lowers his voice to almost a whisper Skylar: "So you know."

Ellie: ",but for the moment let's act like I don't, we're already here and I just want to try being happy, even if it doesn't suit me."

time passes and we ride all the rides at least twice Skylar: "Ellie, let's take a break."

Ellie: "Yeah, I was planning on breaking up with you."

he stares at me forlorn

Skylar: "I meant, take a break from the rides."

Ellie: "Well shit. At least it's out now."

we sit outside the festival on a bench

Ellie: "Yeah sure, It's almost time anyways."

Skylar: "Now's a good time to put on my sweater."

Ellie: "Honestly, I don't want it, I'll feel greedy-"

< Another Perspective >

Skylar: "I did it a lot. It was with many girls, not just with Ava. So take it as an apology."

I didn't want to know that. The more he reminded me made me reject his gifts more. I don't want something reminding me how shitty things are, but I didn't want to go back and forth so I just sat in silence.

Skylar: "Guess you should know that, Say something."

Ellie: "Hello, Whats up."

he smiles a bit sadly Skylar: "Are you upset?"

Ellie: "You tell me, I told you many things I didn't even tell my friends and well.."

Skylar: "Not really your friend..." *he covers his mouth with regret*

Ellie: "Don't be afraid the damage is done. I've always been hurt, but forget it. You're right. I don't know who I'm more hurt by this time. My family is my enemy and so are my so-called friends."

Skylar: "Sorry."

I don't think you are.

Ellie: "We didn't suit well enough anyways, I was always embarrassed of what people thought when they saw us. Now you can roam freely with hotter confident girls who have the loosest parents that can give you action that you so desperately need."

It became silent and he decided to walk away Ellie: "Wait, please."

I didn't care much about looking vulnerable. It didn't matter compared to other things. Things would drift afterwards. Well drift apart, but all I want is to be alone yet next to him. Forget the awkwardness of silence. Our moments were filled with chatter, but look where I'm at. Might as well give silence a chance. There's nothing I can do, I'm corrupt.

Ellie: "No rush. We have the whole world ahead of us to never talk again."

he sits back down and we glare at the sky in silence my mom pulls to the curve and I stand up Skylar: "Are you breaking up with me?"

Ellie: "Yes."

Skylar: "No, you're not."

confused I look back

Ellie: "Yes I am, thanks for that night, I'll remember it till death."

Skylar: "Ellie! I loved you, I was out of it and did something wrong, but I really liked you."

Ellie: "Clearly not enough to respect me."

I've been reciting this in my mind for many times and the time has come to be blunt Ellie: "Did you really, truly love me?"

*his mouth moves but he doesn't speak. He became silent. I wasn't expecting much. Though he decided to uncover the truth, hiis silence was an answer. I just stared until his signals

< Another Perspective >

reached my mind. We just gazed dumbstruck. Until he tries to say something. I increase my hand*

I don't want to hear it.

Skylar: "You never truly loved me either, you're just lonely and desperate for the feeling of someone loving you, but no one did. So technically nothing has changed. Break up with me, never talk to Ava, because you were always empty with or without us."

Ellie: "You don't know me."

Skylar: "I may not, but am I wrong?"

Ellie: "Desperate for love isn't so wrong. Having two people's devoted hearts to yourself and playing with it, that's wrong."

I turn away and start to walk faster as time passes I shouldn't have asked, Why the fuck did I ask.

Don't cry, Don't cry. Don't be so emotional.

I become dulful with a heavy heart as tears come to my eyes.

I really thought he loved me at the time. I wasted all this time for nothing. I made a fucking fool of myself.

Skylar: "Just give me some time to explain myself bitch!"

Ellie: "What the fuck do you wanna say? You had your time to say anything and everything beforehand. You're irrational,"

Skylar: "Maybe you deserve to be depressed. Do all women think they are so perfect?!"

Ellie: "I don't know. Do all men raise their voice to act like their right when they're really wrong. Never said I was perfect."

His expression changed as he darts to me leading me to hastily back up

I'm cornered as his hands clutch to my neck.

I just want to die, wheater its suicide or not. I wish he'd kill me. No one would find out I was a sad girl. Their view one me would stay the same and I'd be out of misery, I'd be great.

The thought of being with someone forever was an escape. It danced around my head. Now you make me want to blow off my head. I'd never think you'd turn out to be like this.

Your face, his face, that's what got me. He soon reminded me of Silas.

I get in the car and lean on the window

Mother: "You shouldn't be hanging with him so much, you should focus on school your young anyways, You'd think I'd be mad but actually I'm realived you're not lesbian-"

I don't feel like arguing. Ellie: "cool."

Mother: "How's school your grades may-"

Ellie: "I have a headache, I'm heading off to bed when we get home."

I was in pain. I did my best to sniffle my urge to cry. Deep breaths, closing my eyes, 'optimistic' thoughts. It didn't work, not even the slightest. I can't stop now. The tears flow, but I

< Another Perspective >

can't let her know. I cover my face with my hair turning to the side with my hand over my eyes.

I turn the volume of the radio

Gospel fills the air. I sulk in the seat hoping the dim lights of the moon doesn't have her noticing the tears that I constantly wipe away. She can't find out. None of my enemies can see me cry. I let my guard down and I became wounded by my once lover. What happens when I'm my own enemy and tell myself to not cry for my own sake, but can't stop. How may I hide from myself? I look at the window reminiscing as a blur of city lights pass. I wasn't meant for this place, this city, this family. This isn't it. It possibly isn't. If it is, what was to be made out of it, This was my downfall from the start.

Mother: "You're not going to eat dinner?"

Ellie: "No thanks, Goodnight."

< Don't expect much >

Ava: "Ellie you can't just leave school like that! They were calling your parents."

Ellie: "I gave them the wrong phone number on purpose for cases like this. Don't state what I can and can't do."

Ava: "What's with the attitude."

we stare in silence

Ellie: "Do you even regret it."

Ava: "Who told you?"

Ellie: "I saw."

Ava: "Oh well, It's not on me. He came for me. You deserve depression, you sad bitch."

Ellie: "You can keep my leftovers."

Ava: "You've changed, for the worst."

Ellie: "We never really knew each other to begin with."

Lucinda: "You guys good?"

Millions of thoughts dancing in my head, I felt rage and wished to strangle her, then it came that feeling of realising I'm really lost. I'm too frustrated to sort anything out, I watched this life fall apart and finally realised this was my own

I had no haven. Where did shit start going this way? Things were better when I didn't date Skylar.

We drifted apart so easily. Everything soon was ruined. School became so awkward and I relied on Lucinda because she was all that's left to fill my void, but I knew she'd leave eventually too.

Ellie: "Don't trip. I knew it, just a matter of time."

Lucinda: "It's not like that. I just can't split my time for two of my friends. If we can't hang like before-"

Ellie: "Don't have her pressuring you. She wants you on her side, I'm sorry I put you in such a shitty position."

Lucinda: "Don't be sorry, Ava shouldn't have done such a thing. I'm just a bit torn. I'll still talk to both of you ever so often. I- I just need a while to not feel- you know sophisticated."

Yeah, I know. Sophisticated. Haven't I been that way all this time?

Imagine how I felt about all this. She must have needed all the time in the world, because she neither talked to me or Ava ever again afterwards.

Go ahead and leave like the others. I knew it, it was only a matter of time. They all leave eventually.

< Another Perspective >

Graye: "Hey, How are things?"

Ellie: "It's great, and you?"

Graye: "Besides the weather at the moment everything is nice. I learn something new everyday. I'll feed you up on it when we meet soon enough."

Ellie: "Ok" I clear my throat from cracking "Can't wait"

Graye: "Give Ava and Lucinda my greetings."

Ellie: "Sure thing."

Graye: "Thanks, and Happy early Birthday."

I press the phone to my chest leading a sigh

Ellie: "Graye, I Miss you."

Graye: "I do too."

Ellie: "Though not to the point where I wanna meet you. You ever think we'll not have any similar interest as we grow older."

Graye: "Even If we change, I'll remember you as before. We may not have much similarities anymore, even hold the blandest conversations. The nostalgia will keep a bond, so don't sound so negative.."

I bite my lip

Ellie: "Everyones been flaking out on me, so please, keep your word. Have a goodnight."

Graye: "I will,'night."

< Bittersweet Sixteen >

Aurora: "Happy Birthday to you."

Turns out Silas had work and couldn't make it, good. Shit just gets shittier as time passes.

Aurora: "You're already 16. Time goes so fast." Not really.

2 more years till I'm 18. I'm almost done with this, though I don't feel it. All this time I've longed to be 18. What if it's worse when I'm an adult? I'll truly have nothing to live for. Even if it gets better. I'll be alone forever. I had one life to live and I lived it like this. If only I redid everything, but who knows if it would have been better.

my eyes well as I blow the candle fastly Aurora: "You alright?"

If only she cared.

I shrug

Ellie: "Tears of Joy I guess."

Aurora: "Did you remind your friends that it's your birthday."

I shake my head

Ellie: "No need to remind them."

Aurora: "Ahah, Did they sing to you and embarrass you."

Ellie: "Of course."

I utterly thought things would be better as time passed. I should have died sooner. Ellie: "Goodbye."

Aurora: "You're not going to eat your cake?"

Ellie: "Maybe tomorrow."

There shouldn't be a tomorrow for me.

Aurora: "Ok then, Set your alarm. Don't be late tomorrow."

Ellie: "Sure thing."

I turn away I headed to the bathroom

shaking I glare at the mirror

Ellie: "2 more years." *I sigh* "2 more years. I'm so close" A year feels much longer than a year.

2 more years. 2 more years. Within 2 years I'll be done. I'll leave this place. Forget everyone. Start over, fix things. Approach everything I've fucked up differently. No one can personally hold me hostage. I can make my own choice for the better or worse.

I'll be happy then... won't I? This is all I can do. The fuck do I expect. I'll be alone. A cardiologist that's studied for 7 years or

< Another Perspective >

more. Feel like leftovers ever so often. I'm better off alone, but I don't want to be. Of course I'll be happy.

I open a cabinet pulling out Ibuprofen What was I thinking?

I swallow the large amount with sink water It's better this way.

Aurora: "Happy 16, Goodnight!"

*she says from downstairs

I slowly smile looking down in the bathroom tears drop to the floor Ellie: "Thanks" *I turn off the lights*

Aurora: "Didn't you set up the alarm." *she says quickly as she barged in*

Ellie: "What, yeah, yeah. Um, my bad." *I place my hand on my head so out of it*

Aurora: "Hurry and change." *she leaves the room*

I change flabbergasted and confused

What the fuck. I'm still alive? I can't succeed in life or die. That's nice to know.

Aurora drops me off and I take my steps on the sidewalk. I walk teetering with my head down. At the corner of my eyes I see Ava and Skylar with blurred vision. I felt a mass wave of heat, but I was shaking. I feel myself getting heavy with shortness of breath

This is weird. I shouldn't be here. I should be dead by now.

*I feel funny, everythings blurry and I begin to fade away.

Everything seemed like it was in slow motion. My Jaw became to shake too as my vision parted I kept looking down at my horrible coordinates trying to walk*

I don't regret it. God, I don't feel well though.

I tried to say something but I was only capable of whispering to myself and even then it was mumbles as I kept stuttering. I took a deep breath with pain in my chest and my mouth parts attempting to say something. I wouldn't know what to say anyways. My knees bend and I feel myself collapse as people stare and Ava rushes to talk to me They call my name numerous times from each and every direction but I can't cope so I close my eyes

No one really cares until you're at the brink; and even then it's just an impulse.

Suicide Hotline: 1-800-273-8255

Instagram: nabisco

Snapchat: ellie_rose4444

Printed in the United States
By Bookmasters